The Emergence of Literacy

)7

I

UKRA Teaching of Reading Monographs

Advisory editor 1986–
Colin Harrison, Lecturer in Education
School of Education, Nottingham University

Partnership with Parents in Reading
Wendy Bloom

Advisory editor 1984–5
Asher Cashdan, Head of Department of Communication Studies,
Sheffield City Polytechnic

The Emergence of Literacy
Nigel Hall

Teaching Information Skills through Project Work
David Wray

Reading: Tests and Assessment Techniques
Second Edition
Peter D. Pumfrey

Children's Writing in the Primary School
Roger Beard

Advisory editors 1977–83
Asher Cashdan
Alastair Hendry, Principal Lecturer in Primary Education,
Craigie College of Education

Listening to Children Reading
Helen Arnold

The Thoughtful Reader in the Primary School
Elizabeth Wilson

The Emergence of Literacy

Nigel Hall

Edward Arnold
A division of Hodder & Stoughton
In association with the United Kingdom Reading Association

© 1987 Nigel Hall

First published in Great Britain 1987
Second impression 1988

British Library Cataloguing in Publication Data

Hall, Nigel
  The emergence of literacy. – (UKRA
  teaching of reading monographs)
  1. Literacy – Great Britain
  I. Title   II. United Kingdom Reading
  Association   III. Series
  302.2'0941   LB1139.R4

ISBN 0-340-40126-4

Typeset by Tradespools Limited, Frome, Somerset
Printed and bound in Great Britain for Edward Arnold, the
educational, academic and medical publishing division of Hodder
and Stoughton Limited, Mill Road, Dunton Green, Sevenoaks,
Kent by Biddles Limited, Guildford and King's Lynn

Contents

Acknowledgments

It would be impossible to thank all of those who have contributed to the creation of this book but I would like to mention some who have helped in particular ways. I am grateful for having had the opportunity to have met and discussed early literacy with Kenneth and Yetta Goodman, Jerry Harste, and John Downing. I must thank Anne Robinson for continual debate and Sally Heap, Gill Keddy, Liz May, Janet Moores, Janette Shearer, and Susan Williams for being wonderfully critical students and superb teachers of literacy. I also thank Barbara Clancy, her staff and, of course, the children from Portwood Nursery School where I was allowed to 'do my own thing' for three months. This book could not have been written without the services of a superb library and I was fortunate indeed in that the librarians at Manchester Polytechnic have been unfailingly helpful and courteous, as well as indefatigable in their pursuit of all kinds of material. I am grateful to Asher Cashdan and Caroline Sheldrick for being possessed of infinite patience; they are probably as surprised as I am that the book is actually finished. Finally, this book would never have been begun had I not been confident of the total and continuous support of my wife.

The authors and publishers would also like to thank Collins for permission to reproduce the extract on pages 17–18 from *Young Children Learning* by Barbara Tizard and Martin Hughes and the National Association for the Teaching of English for permission to use part of Nancy Martin's article 'Encounters with Models' on page 86.

Introduction

This is a book about young children who are becoming literate before they enter formal schooling. It is not a book about how to teach literacy, nor is it about those special children who arrive in the reception class already able to read and write. The concern of this book is with all children growing up in a Western, print-oriented society and the ways in which they make sense of that print experience. It may come as a surprise to some to know that children are making any sense of the experience; after all, they are unlikely to have received any formal instruction about literacy. However, the view that instruction is necessary before anything can be learned about literacy is, although widely believed, far from the truth.

Some gifted teachers have always known that children are much better at constructing their own knowledge than we are at teaching them but it has only been during the last fifteen years that a serious attempt has been made by researchers to understand how children come to develop their own knowledge about literacy. It appears that children are not afraid of enquiring into the way print functions. Just as children observe and think about many features of the world, so they look at, and reflect upon, literate acts. This does not mean that they arrive at school as readers and writers in conventional terms; far from it. But it does mean that most children will arrive at school knowing something about what written language is, how it works, and what it is used for. The nature and the quality of children's early experiences with print will result in their achieving many different levels of knowledge and performance. Whatever the level, its achievement presupposes fundamental understanding about the nature and purpose of print. Unfortunately, the chances of children being able to continue to develop these broad and varied understandings are often limited once they arrive at school.

For most of this century the school literacy curriculum has been criticised as sterile, narrow, distorted and quite unresponsive to the world of print outside school. This book looks at the evidence of research during the last fifteen years and attempts to show how children are making sense of the way literacy works in their culture. I have, where possible, used British research. However, not only is this limited but much of the research which has provided the impetus for the examination of literacy before schooling derives from other countries. In some of those countries children start school later than in Britain and may experience a more formal kindergarten education than would be the case in Britain.

Thus the research quoted in this book sometimes involves children up to the age of six or seven. However, where possible, I have used evidence from studies which involved a broad age range of children and which used children who have received little in the way of formal literacy instruction.

What follows is not an attempt to claim that all children arrive at school as conventional literates, but represents a strong claim that we should be more concerned with valuing the knowledge children have than with replacing it by highly dubious and narrow models of what literacy is and how it functions.

1 The discovery of emergent literacy

INTRODUCTION

The aim of this chapter is to discuss recent views about and research on, the emergence of literacy. It would be incorrect to give the impression that everyone agrees with these views or to suggest that the evidence for these views is fully understood. It is, however, clear that in the last ten years, and particularly during the last five years, considerable effort has been put into investigating the competence of children as literacy learners, and redefining what it means for them to become literate. Researchers from a variety of disciplines have been contributing knowlege which, when put together, provides a powerful image of the child as a competent enquirer into the nature and purpose of literacy. Teachers have also played their part in this revaluation and there are many across the world who are creating classroom environments which reflect this new knowledge. Much of this knowledge is not, of course, completely new – nothing ever is – and this chapter will refer to some earlier thoughts which would be quite acceptable to most recent researchers in this area. However, there are many elements which were not known or understood before the asking of certain kinds of questions became a legitimate activity. If the question, 'When do children become literate?' is answered by the response, 'When they come to school', there is no clear incentive to look at what is happening to children before they arrive at school. Fortunately some researchers have not been restricted by such answers and it is their findings which form the basis for this book.

The Western print environment is the most complex and demanding ever experienced by the human race. All of us who live in it cannot help but be substantially involved in it. The speedy advance of information technology, far from reducing the burden, has added to the complexity. The encroachment of television into our lives has increased the need to read in order for us to see what we wish to view; it has also led to the development of an audience for books related to the programmes. Children, from birth, are witnesses to both the existence of print and the relationship between print and people. It would seem strange, given the way that children involve themselves in all aspects of their world, if anyone suggested that there was one part of that visible world about which children were totally ignorant. Yet that is precisely the assumption that underpins so much conventional instruction. There has been an almost universal assumption that either children are ignorant about the nature and purpose of literacy unless they are 'taught' it, or that what children know is of no importance whatsoever in devising teaching strategies. The overall effect of such views is that there has been a devaluation of children's competence, and an emphasis on direct instructional practices. Ferreiro and Teberosky (1983) put this problem into perspective: 'We have searched unsuccessfully in this literature for reference to children themselves, thinking children who seek knowledge, children we have discovered through Piagetian theory. The children we know are learners who actively try to understand the world around them, to answer questions the world poses... it is absurd to imagine that four or five year old children growing up in an urban environment that displays print everywhere (on toys, on billboards and road signs, on their clothes, on TV) do not develop any ideas about this cultural object until they find themselves sitting in front of a teacher' (p. 12).

CONVENTIONAL ASSUMPTIONS

For most of this century the curriculum for the teaching of literacy skills in Britain and the USA has been based on a number of apparently fundamental assumptions. These are that:

- reading and writing are primarily visual-perceptual processes involving printed unit/sound relationships;

- children are not ready to learn to read and write until they are five or six years old;

- children have to be taught to be literate;

- the teaching of literacy must be systematic and sequential in operation;

- proficiency in the 'basic' skills has to be acquired before one can act in a literate way;

- teaching the 'basic' skills of literacy is a neutral, value-free activity.

These assumptions, albeit sometimes unspoken and implicit, controlled the way most educationalists dealt with literacy. The following quotation from Walcutt (in Goddard, 1974) effectively embodies most of them:

Reading is first of all and essentially the mechanical skill of decoding, of turning the printed symbols into the sounds which are language... We are intensely concerned that our children understand what they read, but the mechanical decoding skill must come first if we are to get them started properly. In the earliest stages of learning to read there is very little need for thinking and reasoning on the part of the child. What he needs is a little practice in mastering a decoding skill and the thinking will come along quite some time later.

t. se ww

Such assumptions did not make the teaching of reading and writing any easier, nor did they resolve the problem of how to teach literacy. They did, however, provide some security; they marked the boundaries of the teacher's task, elevated the status of the teacher, and controlled perception of some of the associated phenomena.

Some of these assumptions clearly gave value to the role of the teacher. The view that children were not ready for literacy until they were five or six years old, and that they had to be taught to be literate, clearly elevates the status of the teacher. Instruction in literacy was a task for the specialist – not the parent.

The fact that reading and writing were perceived as visual/perceptual processes, and that they had to be taught in a systematic and sequential way, enabled the creation of an elaborate set of rules governing the order in which these relationships had to be taught. Once rules were clearly expressed, the teaching of these rules became an activity akin to a science, understood by most teachers to be a neutral, value-free activity. Thus, by applying the rules in a systematic way, children were inevitably supposed to become literate. As these rules became more and more complex and elaborate so the specialist nature of literacy teaching was confirmed. It was the teacher who had the skills and the knowledge – not the child or the parent. As few children were capable of coping with this myriad of specialist-created skills, so the belief in children's literacy incompetence was reinforced. The creation of a complex hierarchy of skills appeared to make it easier to locate and diagnose failure in literacy development. However, too often the failure was a result of the hierarchy. Stories abound of children who were reading conventionally before they arrived at school, but because they failed to identify some key words or recite their alphabet they were classed as non-readers.

Thus, whether the teaching was based on phonic, alphabetic, whole word, or sentence methods of reading instruction, certain elements remained unchanged. Control of the manner and rate of learning was in the hands of the teacher. It was the teacher's task to control the child's development from a state of illiteracy to becoming someone with a mastery of the skills involved in being literate; the child's role was to follow the teacher's route from beginning to end.

As a result of more recent understanding about, and awareness of, literacy, and the ways in which children develop a comprehension of literacy, it is possible to identify a number of features that are not reflected in the above assumptions.

- There was no consideration that becoming a reader and becoming a writer were closely related processes.

- There was no consideration that becoming literate might be a social process and be influenced by a search for meaning.

- There was no consideration that most pre-school children might actually have some knowledge of literacy.

- There was no consideration that becoming literate might be a continuous developmental process that begins very early in life.

- There was no consideration of the organisation and control that children might bring to becoming literate.

- There was no consideration that in order to become literate a child might need to engage in literate acts.

- There was little consideration of how language and stories might inform, in particular ways, children's understandings about literacy and text.

- There was no consideration that the knowledge that children have about literacy might be a legitimate element of their literacy development.

Although conventional assumptions may not reflect such ideas, there are perspectives on the development of literacy which do.

AN HISTORICAL ALTERNATIVE

This chapter is entitled 'The discovery of emergent literacy' but it would be more accurate, in some respects, to write about the 'rediscovery'. In 1898 Miss Harriet Iredell wrote an article which contained a number of thoughts that were diametrically opposed to the assumptions outlined above. Consider the following thoughts from Miss Iredell when reflecting on the development of written and oral language:

> It would seem that not only are the processes alike by their own nature but that the child in all cases where he has access to books and writing materials starts to take to reading and writing as he took to hearing language and talking, his progress being according to conditions furnished, in exceptional cases reaching fruition in the full ability to read and write.

Consider also Miss Iredell's thoughts on certain points in oral language and written language development:

> Scribbling is to writing what babbling is to talking, preceding it, holding the same office of forming the organ, giving practice in shaping the elements. As a babbling child thinks he talks so the scribbling child thinks he writes. One is as natural to him, as universal, as much a part of his growth as the other. He needs no urging to practise either.

And consider finally her views on instruction in literacy:

> We never cease to wonder at the extent and amount of knowledge accumulated during the first three years of life nor at the rate of development of the little creature. We say 'Let this go on through the

first years of school life and what may not be done'. But something bars the way. We are told, 'He must learn to read and write'. As if he had not already taken the first steps, and of his own volition, his efforts unrecognised for what they are.

In that final sentence Miss Iredell neatly encapsulates a contemporary view of emergent literacy. During the last ten years researchers and teachers have identified many of these first steps and have demonstrated what it is that those steps really represent – actual literate behaviour.

The rediscovery and affirmation of emergent literacy was preceded by the recognition of schoolchildren's competence in learning to read. This recognition is attributable to a small number of researchers, namely Marie Clay in New Zealand, Kenneth Goodman in America, and Frank Smith in America and Canada. The work of these researchers and writers does not support the 'rule-bound' and 'teacher-controlled' stance of much literacy education. Unlike many other attacks on the deficit model of literacy education, their views have been sustained and developed, and have, in turn, generated a substantial body of multi-disciplined research which supports their claims.

The work of Clay (collected in Clay, 1982) and Goodman (collected in Gollasch, 1982) demonstrated clearly that children were not allowing themselves to be processed into becoming readers. As Clay (1982, p. xii) says: 'Children supplement the programme with their own efforts'. Both Clay and Goodman worked with children's errors and discovered that the common sense notion of an error being something that was simply wrong was not indicative of the reader's true response. They both found that these errors (which Goodman prefers to call miscues) revealed the considerable efforts being made by children to make sense of the material they were reading. In other words children already had some competence in reading.

Smith (1971) and Goodman (see Gollasch, 1982) both regard reading as a natural language process involving the reader in linguistic, cognitive, and social strategies in order to process print directly for meaning. Smith has also extended these principles to writing (Smith, 1982). Smith and Goodman have redefined literacy by moving away from definitions relating simply to perceptual processes to definitions based on cognitive activity in terms of making sense of print. That 'making sense of print' inevitably involves a social perspective. This conceptualisation of literacy as a meaning-based activity is not itself novel (see Thorndike, 1917, on reading), but what is relatively new is that both Smith and Goodman have applied this belief not only to the way adults engage in literate behaviour but also to the way children approach learning to read and write. They suggest that children approach print in a manner essentially similar to that of adults; children expect print to make sense. They are: 'Seekers after meaning motivated by the need to comprehend' (Goodman and Goodman, 1979) and they claim that children bring to print strategies which assume the usefulness of the medium.

This shift in emphasis clearly has implications for the assumptions identified at the beginning of this chapter. If learning to read and write are 'natural language' processes then can it really be the case that children have to wait until the age of five before they can engage in literacy-based activities? If it is a 'natural language' process then can it be the case that children have to be taught to read and write? Smith (1979) and Goodman, Goodman and Burke (1978) deny emphatically that children have to wait; indeed the basis of their claim, like that of Iredell cited earlier, is that children do not wait. As Goodman and Goodman (1979) put it: 'Children are aware of the functions of print and are adaptive to the characteristics of print.' For Goodman and Smith the view that literacy acquisition was a natural process generated an important question: When does that process begin? With this apparently simple question the investigation of emergent literacy was legitimised.

There were, inevitably, other reasons why researchers began to focus on literacy before schooling. One of these reasons derived from research into metacognitive aspects of learning to read (using thought to reflect on thinking), and another derived from studies of early readers. A whole set of investigations, which appear to begin with Reid (1959), apparently demonstrated that children beginning school have little idea of the purpose and processes of reading. Chapter 5 of this book will look again at some of this research and it is sufficient to say at this point that, whether those researchers were right or wrong, they did focus attention on the knowledge about reading that children brought to school.

Equally important were a number of investigations into 'early readers' as they raised interesting questions about the relationship between knowledge about literacy and pre-school experiences. To some extent studies of early readers are studies of competence. If one believes that most children know nothing about literacy when they arrive at school then those who do must have something of the status of freaks. Psychologists love nothing more than to study the 'abnormal' and consequently there have been many studies of such 'early readers'. However the number of studies and the number of children found who were competent, led Torrey, in a review of such studies (Torrey 1979), to suggest that such competence was more common than had appeared. It was clear from those studies that the early experiences children had with print played a significant role in the emergence of literacy.

The time for an alternative approach seemed right in the light of new conceptualisations of psycholinguistics, the puzzles of the metacognitive research and the insights obtained from studies of early readers. Many researchers and teachers were feeling that terms like 'pre-reading skills' or, presumably, 'pre-writing skills' or 'pre-literacy skills' were unhelpful in describing young children's print-related behaviours. As Holdaway (1979) said: 'When we apply a term like "pre-reading skills" to such behaviour we demean their real status as early literacy skills, for they actually display all the features of mature strategies already achieving sound and satisfying outcomes' (p. 56).

A CURRENT ALTERNATIVE

I began this chapter by considering a number of assumptions contained in conventional literacy instructional strategies. It will be useful to compare those assumptions with those of someone approaching the emergence of literacy from a rather different perspective; a perspective derived from the work of the Goodmans and Frank Smith.

Yetta Goodman has for many years been studying the emergence of literacy. Her specific interest began when some children she was studying failed reading readiness tests. 'Yet even these children were beyond beginning reading. They were doing things and had developed concepts that were part of the reading process of mature proficient readers' (Goodman, 1980, p. 2). This is not unlike a comment made by Clark in her study of young fluent readers (Clark, 1976, p. 32): 'It is possible for even young children to become very fluent readers in spite of an average or below average ability to reproduce, or even to remember in their correct orientation, isolated designs sufficiently clearly to identify them from a range of alternatives.' It also brings to mind the case of Larry Wilson who at the age of four 'Failed a reading readiness test but read material on the second or third grade level' (Krippner, 1963, p. 108).

Yetta Goodman does not accept that reading and writing are primarily visual/perceptual skills involving mainly printed unit/sound relationships. She would not deny that these relationships exist but sees their use as only one, and often a very inefficient, strategy if used in isolation: 'Reading consists of optical, perceptual, syntactic and semantic cycles each melting into the next as readers try to get to meaning as efficiently as possible using minimal time and energy' (Goodman and Goodman, 1979, p. 149). She would reject the view that children cannot be literate until they are five or six years old. She claims that: 'The beginnings of reading development often go unnoticed in the young child... this lack of sensitivity occurs because the reading process is misunderstood, because learning to read print and being taught to read it have been conceived as one-to-one correspondence, and because we have been led to believe that the most common-sense notions about learning to read suggest that it begins in a formalised school setting' (Goodman, 1980, p. 9).

She does not believe that children have to be taught to be literate: 'In an environment rich with written language experiences which have real purpose and function for the children, the concepts and oral language about written language develop over a period of time... given time, children work out for themselves what items belong in what categories' (Goodman, 1980, p. 25). She would not expect the teaching of literacy to be systematic and sequential in operation. She argues: 'It helps educators in understanding the reading process to study what proficient readers do when they read. But it is a serious mistake to create curricula based on artificial skill sequences and hierarchies derived from such studies' (Goodman and Altwerger, 1980 p. 84).

Yetta Goodman would not consider that the basic skills have to be acquired before one can act in a literate way: 'The children we have studied and worked with have received no formal instruction yet they have begun to read. Reading may be its own readiness' (Goodman and Altwerger, 1980, p. 84). She does believe that literacy is anything but a neutral, value-free activity. She claims that it is: 'Impossible to consider literacy development without understanding the significance of literacy in the culture – in both the larger society in which a particular culture grows and develops and within the specific culture in which the child is nourished' (Goodman, 1980, p. 4).

Most of the above responses are concerned with the reading process, but it is clear that Goodman accepts that those beliefs apply equally to writing. Her position is summed up when she says: 'My research has shown that literacy develops naturally in all children in our literate society' (Goodman, 1980, p. 31). There would appear to be a number of fundamental assumptions behind the above statements which are rather different from those underpinning more conventional beliefs about literacy:

- Reading and writing are cognitive and social abilities involving a whole range of meaning-gaining strategies.

- Most children begin to read and write long before they arrive at school. They do not wait until they are 'taught'.

- Literacy emerges not in a systematic, sequential manner, but as a response to the printed language, and social environment experienced by the child.

- Children control and manipulate their literacy learning in much the same way as they control and manipulate all other aspects of their learning about the world.

- Literacy is a social phenomenon and as such is influenced by cultural factors. Therefore the cultural group in which children grow up will be a significant influence on the emergence of literacy.

In essence Goodman proposes a model of literacy development where the child is a competent cognitive and social learner who can develop, on his/her own, knowledge about, and abilities with, literacy. The child is seen as having competence to learn by living in a world where phenomena can have meaning assigned to them. This is, clearly, quite different from the assumptions embedded in conventional instruction, particularly with regard to very young children (see Walker, 1975).

Goodman has, on several occasions, used the word 'natural' to describe the way children become literate. It is a term which has been used by a number of other writers (Curtis, 1984; Forester, 1977; Hoskisson, 1979; Malicky and Norman, 1985; Schmidt and Yates, 1985; Stine, 1980; Teale, 1982 and 1984; and Torrey, 1979). It is, however, rather an awkward word, for what counts as 'natural' may vary between people. For many, the word 'natural' implies some kind of maturational phenomenon; something that occurs almost inevitably as a result of biological programming. However, in defining learning to read and write as natural processes, neither Smith nor the Goodmans are suggesting that there is some kind of biological mechanism operating; they are not suggesting an alternative literacy acquisition device (LAD). They are claiming that literacy is learnt in much the same way, and to some extent at the same time as, oral language. Both oral language and literacy development are dependent on an appropriate context for the 'natural' development of those skills. People use language and literacy in the pursuit of their everyday lives. In other words, within such contexts people engage in literacy and oracy in order that they may continue to experience the satisfaction of human needs.

Children would not learn to talk if deprived of access to purposeful oral language use. No child has ever learnt to talk by being locked in a room with an endless supply of tape-recorded language. Children have to experience language being used by people in appropriate ways, and appropriate ways are those which enable the creation of meanings and the sharing of meanings. In the same way, no child would ever learn to read if locked into the British Library. Children must have access to people using print in appropriate ways. Thus the 'naturalness' is a function of social experiences where literacy is a means to a variety of other ends.

Of course, within such environments all kinds of people – adults, siblings, and friends – help children in their learning. However, this seldom takes place as a result of systematic and sequential instructional practices; it is a consequence of playing and living with children. The same effects can be found in literacy development (Gundlach et al., 1985). It is the literacy development within these contexts that Goodman and others are labelling 'natural'.

Recently a term has become current which is, perhaps, more useful and less ambiguous than the word 'natural' in describing the way young children develop literacy competencies. It is, perhaps, more helpful to talk about literacy 'emerging' within certain kinds of contexts. Sulzby (1985) has used the term 'emergent' to describe this behaviour. She recognised that although children below the age of six are demonstrating literate behaviour it is, for the most part, not yet the same in its totality as conventional reading and writing. However, this rather begs the question of what can be described as 'conventional' reading and writing. The term has also been used by Holdaway (1979) but like Sulzby he uses the term within a stage theory of the development of literacy. Holdaway has 'emergent reading' followed by 'advanced emergent reading' and then by 'emergent to early reading'. (It is interesting to note that although Holdaway's book is titled *The Foundations of Literacy*, his stages are still labelled with the term 'reading'.) The difficulty with stage theories of emergent literacy is that it is too easy to find children who appear to be at several stages at once.

The word 'emergent' is, however, useful on four counts. First, it implies that development takes place from within the child. Even though people may inform children about many aspects of literacy, responsibility for making sense of all the data rests with the child. Therefore instruction is not the only means of encouraging the emergence of literacy. Secondly, 'emergence' is a gradual process: it takes place over time. Thirdly, for something to emerge there has to be something there in the first place. Where emergent literacy is concerned this means the fundamental abilities children have, and use, to make sense of the world; abilities demanded by both Piagetians (Ferreiro and Teberosky, 1983) and sociologists (Harste *et al.*, 1984). Fourthly, things usually only emerge if the conditions are right. Where emergent literacy is concerned that means in contexts which support, facilitate enquiry, respect performance and provide opportunities for engagement in real literacy acts.

Thus in this book the word 'emergent' is preferred to the word 'natural', although the meaning is much the same as implied by Goodman's (1980) use of the latter term. The use of the term 'emergent' in this book does not imply the requirement of a culturally universal, systematic developmental sequence as Sulzby and Holdaway seem to be suggesting. Indeed they may not subscribe at all to my definition of 'emergence'. It is, however, the preferred definition of this book and the purpose of the following chapters is to consider how and when literacy emerges, and what form it takes.

2 The linguistic and social background of emergent literacy

INTRODUCTION

The assumptions which underlie the approach to emergent literacy outlined in the previous chapter represent explicit claims about literacy being a language process. As a language process it is, like oral language, rooted in the social relationships experienced by people. As Harste *et al.* (1984) remind us: 'Language, whether oral or written, is a social event of some complexity. Language did not develop because of the existence of one language user but of two' (p. 28).

There have been many, and various, claims about the relationship between learning to use oral language and learning to use written language. The relationship being considered in this book is that between learning oral language, and learning about written language. The claim being made is not about the relationship between learning oral language and children's responses to instruction about written language. In the past children's responses to the teaching of literacy were confounded with how literate knowledge and abilities emerged during childhood. Thus learning about literacy was seen almost solely as a function of teaching about literacy. Indeed the assumptions outlined at the beginning of Chapter 1 presumed that literacy could only be a response to instruction. As a consequence, even when researchers looked at the relationship between Piagetian stages and literacy, they tended to consider the relationship in terms of educator-generated sub-skills and those stages, rather than look at the way children made sense of literacy (Elkind, 1981). Such attitudes are indicative of a belief that reading and writing have to be taught and are therefore qualitatively different from speaking and listening which, the belief goes, do not have to be taught. Coltheart reviews the notion of reading readiness and demonstrates that as a concept it has no basis in fact. However, he quite categorically asserts that 'Reading does not appear spontaneously' and that 'If a child is not taught to read then he will never be able to do it, no matter how mature he is' (Coltheart, 1979, p. 16). Such a conclusion seems extraordinary, as by 1979 there were many studies of children who had arrived at school already able to read; indeed he even makes use of such a study. The book in which his article appeared also included a lengthy paper which did nothing but review such studies (Torrey, 1979).

The ways in which the relationship between oral language learning and written language learning has been perceived have changed as knowledge of human behaviour has changed. Wardaugh (1969) reviewed the literature and came to the conclusion that 'Reading acquisition seems to be very different from language acquisition, and the theories of language acquisition appear to have little to offer anyone in coming to a better understanding of how beginning reading should be taught' (p. 1). It is interesting to note that again the demand was for oral language development to inform directly the 'teaching' of reading. For some reason it was appropriate to investigate oral language acquisition as learning in its own right but it was only appropriate to examine written language acquisition in terms of how it could be taught. If Wardaugh's conclusion seems somewhat pessimistic it is mostly because the evidence he reviewed did not allow him to take another view.

Only two years later, Smith, reviewing a different set of evidence, was able to take a different stance: 'Many of the skills employed by a child in learning about speech are relevant to the task of learning to read' (Smith, 1971, p. 2). Smith, it should be noted, does not use the word 'teach' but the word 'learn'.

THE EMERGENCE OF ORAL LANGUAGE IN CONTEXT

Linguists and psychologists in the 1960s were primarily interested in the acquisition of the phonological and grammatical features of language. This meant that language was, in a sense, being studied apart from its primary function – communication between human beings. For researchers at that time the study of the use of language was the study of how individuals were able to generate phonology and grammar. It did not examine how those aspects were used in social interaction for communicative purposes, or how language was used in order to enable people to live their lives. Once one begins to look at oral language from a more functional point of view it becomes apparent that there are many real similarities between acquiring an understanding of oral language and acquiring an understanding of written language.

It is the work of the linguist Halliday which has had most impact on reassessing the way in which children learn language. He says: 'Learning one's mother tongue is learning the use of language, and the meanings, or rather the meaning potential, associated with them. The structures, the words and the sounds are the realisation of this meaning potential. Learning language is learning how to mean' (Halliday, 1973, p. 24).

According to Halliday, it is through learning how to mean that other aspects of language are acquired. It was one of Cazden's paradoxes of language acquisition that while parents and children attended to meaning, the structure was nevertheless learnt. Halliday claims that children do not attend to language as an atomistic, structural phenomenon as most children are expected to when they are taught to read; children are concerned with making sense because it is making sense that enables life to be lived. Thus to talk of language is to talk of the social situation within which meanings are generated. As Halliday points out: 'What is common to every use of language is that it is meaningful, contextualised, and in the broadest sense social; this is brought home very clearly to the child, in the course of his day-to-day experience. The child is surrounded by language, but not in the form of grammars and dictionaries, or of randomly chosen words and sentences, or of undirected monologue. What he encounters is "text", or language in use: sequences of language articulated each within itself and within the situation in which it occurs. Such sequences are purposive – though very varied in purpose – and have an evident social significance' (p. 20).

A child's development in language occurs through the attempt to engage in communicative acts – both as a producer and a receiver. A child's life is accompanied by language but this language itself exists to permit other functions of life to occur. It is relatively rare for young children to experience language itself as a focus of language except within formal instruction, i.e. using language to *examine* language, whether spoken or written.

Most of the language that children experience is embedded in the pursuit of other ends: demanding objects or actions; controlling people and events; mediating relationships; developing a concept of self; asking questions about the world; extending reality through imagination; and informing others. Language is not the focus of these interactions; it is a medium for fulfilling objectives and as such it is somewhat transparent. The child looks through language and sees the social function of the interaction. It is for this reason that children become users, indeed proficient users of language, without achieving what has come to be called linguistic awareness, i.e. an understanding of what language is, rather than an understanding of how it is used.

It could be inferred from Halliday's work that any child brought up in an environment where oral language is not related to social functioning will not be able to talk. It is difficult to conceive of circumstances occurring wherein children are mechanically maintained and subject to long hours of tape-recorded language. It is conceivable that they might imitate some of the sounds but those sounds would not enable them to perform as language users. What is a necessary condition of language learning is the existence of a context where children can grow surrounded by purposeful and meaningful use of language. The facilitators in such situations are other people who not only use language purposefully, but respond to the child as if he were an appropriate user of language.

For most children in Western society oral language is learnt in the home through interaction with parents, siblings and close relations. Without their language degenerating into atomised fragments they provide support and encouragement as the children flex their linguistic muscles. Wells suggests that 'what is most important in the behaviour of children's parents and other caretakers is sensitivity to their [the children's] current state – their level of communicative ability and their immediate interests – and to the meaning intentions they are endeavouring to communicate; also a desire to help and encourage them to participate in the interaction' (Wells, 1985, p. 69).

Parents do adjust their speech when interacting with young children (a form which has been labelled 'motherese') and this talk is: 'characterised by formal simplicity, fluent and clear delivery and high redundancy in context' (Wells, 1985, p. 65). Parents engage in rituals with their children which have been variously called 'scaffolds' and 'formats' by Bruner (1985). A format or a scaffold is essentially a framework within which children and adults can engage in specific types of linguistic behaviour. They are, to some extent, in a safety net. Within this 'safety net' the child can play around with the roles of the participants, practise roles, repeat roles, and ultimately move beyond the safety net to use the newly-learned abilities in other situations. Games like 'peekaboo' can be such a 'scaffold' for learning how aspects of language are used, and how the respective participants in the game use their language to control how the game moves and progresses.

In addition to 'scaffolding' linguistic behaviours, parents also show children what talk is for. Cazden says: 'As we talk to children, how we speak indicates how texts are constructed for particular purposes and in particular situations' (Cazden, 1983, p. 11). Children from an early age seem competent to follow conversation between adults by shifting their gaze as each person speaks. The force of these demonstrations clearly increases during the first years of life as children experience their parents coming into contact with a wide range of siblings, friends, shopkeepers and so on.

Two important points must be understood. The first is that the above aspects appear to give the parent the role of instructor. Such 'instruction' bears little relationship to the instruction of schooling. Parents are most unlikely to be instructing in the sense of formulating specific teaching objectives and devising strategies to achieve these objectives. Rather, parents are respondents and participants. Tizard and Hughes (1984) wrote of their study into the home language of young children: 'Some mothers turned games and stories to educational advantage, while a few gave their children formal "lessons". But in most families these occasions were relatively rare' (p. 73). Most studies of young child-adult interaction show that it is usually the child who initiates and terminates the action rather than the parent. The mainly unconscious devices of the parents enable them to follow, extend, elaborate, participate, and create opportunities for language use. Wells claims that adults 'are intuitively aware that the major responsibility for actually mastering the resource of their language rests with the child rather than with themselves and that their role is essentially one of sustaining and encouraging the child's self-activated learning'. (Wells, 1985, p. 71).

The second point is that this encouragement, support, and facilitation is usually not focused on the mastering of linguistic skills. It is, as has previously been indicated, focused on the pursuit of other activities and the linguistic exercise is embedded within the achievement of those pursuits. Thus games are played not for instruction but because both the child and the parent get pleasure from playing them. Most conversations derive from living an everyday existence which demands cleaning, cooking, shopping, dressing, sleeping and so on. As Tizard and Hughes put it: 'One of our strongest impressions from this study was the amount children learned from simply being around with their mothers; discussing what each was doing, or had done, what they could do next, arguing with each other, and, above all, endlessly asking and answering questions' (Tizard and Hughes, 1984, p. 73). Even when parents do play a kind of instructional game, for example, 'point to your nose', the emphasis is, in incidents that I have observed, less on the linguistic proficiency and more on the knowledge of the body: parents are pleased because the child has learned where its nose is, rather than because the child can understand the linguistic nature of the question.

Because these interactions are based around some form of social activity, language and culture are intimately linked; indeed language is the culture. By being a participant in language interaction, the child is learning not just about the forms and uses of language but about the world mediated by that language. As Wells puts it: 'Just as children learn the language system through experience of using it as a resource, so in increasing their control of the resources of language they also increase their understanding of the experiences embedded by those resources' (Wells, 1985, p. 71), and, of course, a great many of those experiences are related to literacy.

From this brief summary of some of the conditions under which oral language emerges, certain principles seem clear:

- Children play the major role in constructing their knowledge of oral language.

- Parents and caregivers greatly facilitate but seldom instruct children in oral language.

- The child is exposed to oral language which is embedded in the pursuit of non-linguistic ends.

- The drive to linguistic competence is the attempt to comprehend and create meanings.

- The conditions for becoming orate are the same as those conditions necessary for developing knowledge of the world.

- Becoming orate depends on social interaction.

- The functions of language understood by children allow them to regulate many aspects of their lives and in turn understand the regulation of their lives by others.

- The experience of language is primarily holistic and any segmented linguistic events that occur are usually the result of child initiation.

THE EMERGENCE OF LITERACY IN CONTEXT

The question now becomes: 'In what ways are the conditions under which children learn about literacy similar to those for learning about oral language?' Are the above principles unique to oral language development or can they be shown to be major factors in the emergence of literacy?

It would seem that if the development of oral language can be seen as a process of learning how to mean, then it becomes possible to see very clear relationships between the emergence of oral language and the emergence of literacy. Literacy, like oral language, exists so that meanings can be created and so that communication can take place between human beings. Literacy events, like oral language events, are mostly explicitly, or implicitly, social. Literacy events are, like oral language events, experienced as meaningful and are usually experienced as means to various ends. Most importantly, literacy, like oral language, is experienced as having many uses and functions because it enables the achievement of that variety of ends.

Literacy in the Western world is a fact of everyday existence. To awake and find all print removed from the environment would be an unnerving experience. Literacy appears for many to be addictive. People take print everywhere. We take books on holidays to distant places and may even, like Somerset Maugham, carry a bag of books with us. On holiday we feel deprived if we cannot get our daily newspaper, and many people cannot sit in a room without their eyes gravitating towards print in any form. Most of us even carry around significant amounts of print in our pockets and on our clothes. As Leichter (1984) reminds us: 'Print does not merely reside in a household but rather flows through it' (p.40). Everyday new print appears and old print is thrown away or recycled to other (sometimes non-print) uses. Just as most oral language is heard and lost, so most print is seen and lost. Only a relatively small amount of print is ever saved. However, just as oral language controls and in turn enables us to control our lives and the lives of other, so print can regulate and transform existence.

One cannot opt out of the Western print world. Even adult illiterates have strategies for enlisting help in understanding print; although they may not be able to read it, they are acutely aware of its power and uses. Families which decline to read books do not opt out of the print world. They may still write and receive letters and notes, look at television guides, glance at comics and magazines, receive junk mail and circulars, read labels, follow instructions, buy postage stamps, have print on T-shirts, be given tickets of all kinds, have to fill in forms, collect coupons, receive wage slips, and so on. The failure of many people, both researchers and teachers, to recognise the extent of such activity in bookless homes is a tribute to the ability of print to hide itself within the pursuit of other ends. Indeed so well hidden are some of the literacy-oriented events in homes that Leichter, when commenting on a study of family homes as environments for literacy, noted that the researchers at first overlooked the print displayed on television. As she says: 'Locating literacy events in the stream of everyday family activities is a substantial task, especially if one wishes to avoid defining literacy in terms of previously held conceptions' (Leichter, 1984, p.42).

A literary act is rarely the function of a family activity. Schieffelin and Cochran-Smith (1984) observed adults and children in a Philadelphia community. They say: 'Literacy events consistently were embedded within the routine social interactions of adults and children. For participants the literacy events themselves were not noteworthy' (p. 7). Equally Anderson and Stokes (1984) who studied literacy events in the homes of very poor families claimed: 'Our data indicate that literacy events function not as isolated bits of human activity but as connected units embedded in a functional system of activity generally involving prior, simultaneously occurring, and subsequent units of action' (p. 28).

Children's experience of literacy is, for the most part, experience of literacy as part of a complete event. The focus is on the complete event or on the aim of the event. Of course, situations do occur where the focus is directly on the nature of the literacy, just as in oral language the focus can be on the language. Parents do buy alphabet books or other instructional books, particularly as children approach formal schooling. Children themselves often initiate print-focused events, for instance when asking, 'What does that say?' or when they begin to recognise features of their own names. However, the overriding impression is of literacy as part of a larger, more meaningful event and this is reflected in their play. 'Ponch' wrote tickets for parking violations (Kammler, 1984), the children in the Hall et al. study (1986) wrote to record orders in their restraurants, Paul Bissex wrote to gain his mother's attention (Bissex, 1980), and the children of Trackton read in order to buy groceries (Heath, 1983). A particularly clear example of the way in which literacy is embedded in other activities was recorded by Tizard and Hughes (1984). They reproduce a transcript of a conversation between a mother and her child. The mother had been making a shopping list and was discussing it with the child:

Mother We've only got that little bit of shopping to get now (shows Pauline the list).
Child Mummy? Can I have one of them drinks? Can I?
Mother Get some more drink?
Child Yeah. Can write it down on there (points to where she wants it written on the list). Up here.
Mother I'll get you some when I go tomorrow.
Child Aw! (disappointed)

Mother All right? Cause I'm not getting it today.
Child No … In the 'Vivo's?
Mother Haven't got Daddy's money yet.
Child I've got no money.
Mother No, I haven't got enough to get my shopping. All of it.
Child Not all of it?
Mother Irene's just taken five pounds. She'll bring some change back. If she's got some, she'll bring some change back. It's not enough to get all that. Is it? (points to the shopping list)
Child No.
Mother See? So when daddy gets paid I'll get some more money and then I'll go and get the rest.
Child Yeah. That's nice, isn't it, Mum?
Mother Mm … I got one, two, three, four, five, six, seven, eight, nine, ten, eleven, twelve (counts items on list).
Child (Joins in counting) Nine, ten, eleven.
Mother Fourteen, fifteen, sixteen, seventeen, eighteen bits.
Child Mum, let's have a look! (Mother shows the child the list) Do it again.
Mother We gotta get rice, tea, braising steak, cheese, pickle, carrots, fish, chicken, bread, eggs, bacon, beefburgers, beans … Oh Irene's gone to get them (crosses off beans) … peas, ham, corned beef.
Child And what's that (points to word on the list)?
Mother That's lemon drink (crosses off 'lemon drink'). She's just gone down to get that one. See?   (Tizard and Hughes, 1984, p.74–5.)

This is a very complex episode. A whole range of factors are embedded in the creation of a shopping list. One can see that counting activities and a lot of work in 'economics' are involved. However, a number of literacy-related events also occur. The child witnesses that a written list is a useful way of organising and planning events; that one can redraft written language; that written language is composed of elements; that one can refer back to a written list for information; that there is a relationship between written and oral language. This family was classed by the researchers as working-class, and they comment: 'It is often suggested that working-class children do not have much experience of their parents engaging in "literate" activities: yet a shopping list provides an extremely vivid demonstration of the way in which written language may be used within a meaningful human activity. The power of the written word lies in its ability to link up different contexts in space or time, and here it is doing precisely that – forming a link between the home, where the decisions and choices are made, and the shop, where they are carried out. The list can also cope with sudden changes of plan – a friend offering to do some of the shopping leads to some items being crossed off the list. The activity is thus not only emotionally but intellectually more powerful than the labelling of pictures, which is likely to be Pauline's introduction to writing when she starts at infant school' (p. 76).

In oral language emergence the role of parent or caregiver is extremely important, not as an instructor but as a facilitator, through discussion, play and demonstration. Within the field of emergent literacy such behaviour is most evident in book-reading episodes. Book-reading episodes have been extensively studied, mostly because they are fairly obvious and self-contained manifestations of literacy experience. However, it may well be the case that an abundance of similar facilitative behaviour could be found in all the other activities of everyday life, just as in the example already cited from Tizard and Hughes. It must not be assumed that parent-child book-reading episodes are phenomena to be observed in all homes in Western society (see Heath, 1982 and Chapter 3 of this book), nor must it be assumed that within smaller cultural groups story reading is carried out in similar ways. Some views on the consequences of book-reading are outlined in Chapter 3 but here it is the nature of the interaction that will be considered. It appears that within many of the mainstream book-sharing sessions, parents extensively modify their practices and behaviour. As Diehl-Faxon and Dockstader-Anderson (1985) say of their study, it 'suggests that not only does the mother model "book-reading talk" which is finely tuned to the child's language ability but she is also fine-tuning her reading to the child's experiential background. This fine-tuning to the child's background is demonstrated by the mother's characteristic use of familiar intonation patterns to emphasise aspects of meaning. These intonational patterns or readerese are similar to patterns found in motherese, and we suggest that mothers use them for similar purposes, to ensure communication, and to facilitate the child's comprehension of meaning' (p. 304).

Snow (1983) identified three characteristics of parent language behaviour which occurred not only in book-reading but in other literacy events. She terms them 'semantic contingency', 'scaffolding' and 'accountability procedures'. When using semantic contingency, adults continue topics previously introduced by children. Snow says examples of semantic contingency would include: 'Answering questions about letter and number names, answering questions about words, reading out loud on request, answering questions about pictures in books, carrying on coherent conversations with children about the pictures and text in books, and giving help with writing when requested' (p. 168). Snow also found scaffolding of literacy events. The mother in her study extensively scaffolded, for her child, the task of spelling his name 'Nathaniel' by 'reminding him of what they were doing, rejecting false starts and guiding letter search' (p. 170). In this way she constrained the task to allow the child greater success. In 'accountability procedures' the mother makes demands that the task be completed, or that the child displays knowledge that it is known to possess. These three procedures then are not only typical of oral language interaction but also of the interactions which surround literacy events.

Parents also frequently act as demonstrators of literacy behaviour, not necessarily in simple or self-evident ways. Through the construction of literacy events parents can reveal many of the more subtle ways in which literacy controls, stimulates and facilitates human behaviour. Leichter offers an example of how a mother, through maintaining a notice board, provided a wide-ranging and powerful demonstration of how literacy works:

> Their bulletin board, largely maintained by the mother, used print to organise the family's life in terms of its basic concerns. An ERA (Equal Rights Amendment) button, newspaper clippings, and cartoons were reflections and reminders of the mother's newly-acquired political and feminist beliefs. A green plastic shamrock and some St Patrick's Day cards were a display and reminder of the family's ethnic identity. Cards for other holidays served to organise and reinforce other ceremonial events within the calendar year. An envelope for coupons and an unemployment book were reminders of the economic realities of the family's life. An appointment card for visits to the pediatrician and dry cleaning slips helped to organise memory. The eldest daughter's successful school report and her scores in a bowling tournament in which she did particularly well attested to special achievements of the family members. Notes of apology or notes saying 'I love you' reinforced relationships or attempted to ease inter-personal problems. Wedding pictures, pictures of family friends, and a card that the daughter had drawn for her mother served to commemorate special occasions. Fliers, posters, pamphlets, leaflets, and notes telling of school board elections, plays, athletic events, and children's entertainment helped the family keep track of community events (p. 44).

Leichter offers a wry comment on schooling when she adds: 'It is difficult to compare the literacy skills involved in clippings, organising, and placing coupons on a bulletin board, or in designing a poster to celebrate a family event, with those involved in filling in blanks in a vocabulary notebook' (Leichter, 1984, p. 45).

Young children's behaviour often shows that they are not simply imitating people around them. When collecting children's accounts of learning to read I found two children who remembered a time before they could 'read'. They told me: 'When I couldn't read I pretended I could read and so everybody thought I was grown up' and: 'I used to pick up my Dad's thick books and sit down and I would flick through the book slowly, pretending to read just looking at the pictures. I used to love doing this. It made me feel big and proud of myself.' Those two children clearly were not simply imitating even though their knowledge had come about partly as a result of observation. Those children had identified what reading looked like, had identified it as a distinct kind of activity, had identified it as an important activity and had identified being able to read as an achievement to be proud of. For them, being literate had social status and was a desirable goal. Thus the activity of 'pretending' to read was actually a more reflective response than simply a crude imitation of an act observed.

CONCLUSION

If the principles outlined on pages 15–16 of this chapter are reviewed, it will be clear that many of them apply equally to the way literacy emerges: parents facilitate the emergence of both oral language and literacy but seldom do it through direct instruction; the child's experience of both oral language and literacy is of that language and literacy embedded in other objectives; children experience oral and written language in similar ways to their experience of other aspects of the world; and the child's experience of oral language and literacy is essentially holistic. This does not, however, account for all the principles identified earlier. The rest will be covered in the next three chapters.

3 The emergent reader

INTRODUCTION

Learning to read and learning to write are closely related activities. Indeed it is difficult to see how one could author a text unless one was able to read it as well. It is, however, convenient to discuss reading and writing in separate chapters. The fact that they are dealt with in this way is simply a convenience of authorship, not an exemplification of their distinctness. Although each chapter has its focus, it is often the case that the link between the two processes is implicit.

This chapter focuses on two aspects of emergent literacy: the understanding of environmental print and the understanding of continuous text, usually in the form of stories. Few children in the Western world will grow up in an environment devoid of print, but some children may be without experience of continuous text. The importance of access to both of these aspects of reading will be examined as well as their significance for the emergence of the child as a conventional reader.

ENVIRONMENTAL PRINT

In Chapter 1 a claim was made about the intensity of the print environment experienced by young children. A more important claim of Chapter 2 was that children interact with this print environment and that the knowledge gained contributes to the development of literacy. Such learning is not apparent in a recent article by Dawson (1984). Dawson is writing about pre-reading skills but, in this article, in the context of environmental awareness. Essentially Dawson's article is a plea for teachers to take into account the environment when considering how to help their children become readers. The article, however, has nothing to say about the print-rich environment experienced by young children in their everyday lives. Dawson's view is that the 'reading process demands a physical and sensory commitment' (p. 18). The 'areas' that form her 'pre-reading programme' (and the word 'programme' is an informative one) are: 'form perception'; 'motor control'; 'visual copying'; 'visual recall'; 'completion and closure'; 'visual rhythm'; 'visual sequencing'; 'temporal sequencing'; 'visual discrimination'; and 'auditory discrimination'. According to Dawson: 'These provide a basic framework of activities to encourage the development of the necessary skills required before a child is able to begin a formal reading programme' (p. 19). Thus Dawson's activities rest on the same fundamental assumptions that underlie conventional attitudes to the development of literacy. The most interesting aspect of Dawson's article is what it does not contain. Nowhere in the article is the word 'print' mentioned. Nor are there any other words relating to actual literate behaviour. Dawson's world seems devoid of print and there is nothing in the article which would help a child to become aware of what literacy is or how it works. The nature and purpose of environmental print could not be made evident from a world bound by such notions of 'pre-reading' skills.

It is sad that an article clearly aimed at teachers helping children learning to read should emphasise such ideas at the expense of using the environment to actually help children learn more about literacy. The evidence is extremely clear and consistent. Young children do pay attention to the literacy-based elements of their environment. They do not ignore them; they use them and by using them continue to construct their views about how print functions. The world of environmental print is a vast resource for children to look at and think about. The term 'environmental print' is, in some respects, an ambiguous one as clearly all print in the world could be construed as being in the environment. However, for the purposes of this chapter it is restricted to exclude, as far as possible, the world of print in books. In general the term is used to refer to those items of print outside the home or deriving from outside the home and to which there is some kind of public or general access. These distinctions are not absolute and are not made because they exist as such in the world, but because other elements are dealt with more conveniently elsewhere in this book. Environmental print is usually thought of as 'contextualised' print. This means that the meaning of the print is, to a large extent, self-evident from the context surrounding the print, for example, the words 'fish and chips' above a fish and chip shop. Decontextualised print is most easily thought of as the continuous text in books which is usually read without the presence of the objects or events to which it relates. It might, however, be useful to remember that so-called contextualised print is not always as 'contextualised' as it might appear. Take a walk down your high street and look at all the environmental print. Is it all contextualised? Are advertisements, whether on hoardings or on the sides of buses, examples of contextualised or decontextualised print? It will be helpful to bear that issue in mind as you read this chapter.

Children do look carefully at their environment. Lass (1982) noticed that her two week old child was staring at her printed T-shirt. Her husband claimed that the child was reading the *New Yorker* at ten weeks: 'Amazingly Jed was scanning the printed matter of the full page advertisements. His eyes swept over the words in a left to right progression. Saccades and return sweeps were evident but naturally the regressions characteristic of reading for understanding were absent' (p. 20). Lass was not, you will be reassured to know, making a serious claim that her child was reading but it was certainly a serious claim that her child was already looking hard and noticing features of the print environment. However at seventeen months Jed was pointing to letters and labelling them all 'B' or 'D'. Baghban's daughter, Giti, clearly distinguished print when twenty months old. 'She continued to maintain her "book babbling" whenever she was not interested in labelling an item in a book or magazine. She applied this activity to her books, our books, fourth class mail, credit cards, billboards and license plates but never with non-print items' (Baghban, 1984, p. 29). Cecilia, Payton's child (Payton, 1984) was also very young when she gave the first indications that she had absorbed messages about the function of print: 'She and I were queueing at the checkout in the supermarket and as I emptied the contents of the basket onto the counter, Cecilia indicated the writing on the ticket and correctly remarked, "that say Coop"' (p. 28). Payton pointed out the significance of this event. As far as was known Cecilia had never previously asked, or even been shown, the word. The only way Cecilia could have learned the word was in the context of conversations about shopping activities. Thus Payton claims: 'The child hypothesised, analysed and finally formulated a proposal' (p. 28).

Frank Smith describes, and many readers will have seen ('How do you read?' BBC *Horizon* programme, 1975), how he took Matthew aged 3½ on a trip around a supermarket and a department store: 'There were a few words that Matthew could read on sight and a number that he got wrong, such as "corn flakes" when the package he was looking at gave a brand name. But he knew a good deal about what the print ought to say on a package label' (Smith, 1976, p. 298). Smith's point is not that Matthew could read in the conventional sense of accurate word identification – clearly he could not – but it was apparent that Mathew did know that words 'said' something and that 'something' was expected to make sense. He understood that printed words had a communicative function and he attempted, on the basis of contextual information, to assign to the word an appropriate meaning. Smith hypothesised that his ability was learned from watching television as commercials frequently present words many times in both written and spoken forms. This is a possibility. After all, Torrey (1969) described how a four year old child learned to read almost solely from watching TV.

Mason (1965) investigated the words that children learned from commercial TV. The few kindergarteners in his test (who, he admits, were all above average in ability) revealed that they had learned a great many words. He concluded: 'Testing of kindergarteners indicates that some children who have had no formal instruction in reading have learned to identify printed words frequently shown and pronounced simultaneously on television' (p. 320). Jones and Hendrickson (1970) in their investigation of 'Recognition by children of advertised products' also found that young children did recognise some words seen on TV commercials. In all three age groups (3, 4 and 5 year olds) products were identified more frequently than book covers. However, Jones and

Hendrickson admit that children are exposed to products from many sources other than TV. The evidence from these studies is, on the whole, ambiguous and it is difficult to agree with Smith that young children's knowledge about environmental print derives almost entirely from watching TV. It certainly may play a part but how much more powerful is the notion of Shirley Payton discussing with her daughter Cecilia what they needed to buy, where they would find it, and then looking and locating the products on the shelves, or the example of Pauline and her mother (cited in Chapter 2) compiling their shopping list. Given the evidence already cited in Chapter 2, the importance of TV in the child's print environment is probably limited, except perhaps in the case of very attractive objects such as toys.

The evidence that a great many children make use of environmental print is overwhelming. Study after study has shown young children who have competencies with contextualised print. Clark (1976) in her study of early readers claims that it was boys who paid most attention to print in the environment. It was: 'The boys who showed interest in signposts, car names, captions on television and names on products at the supermarket' (p. 51). This sexual difference has not, as far as I can tell, been reported by any other researcher. Evidence of the extent of use of print, other than books, is related by Schickedanz and Sullivan (1984) who reported that 75% of the three hundred literacy events noted by the researchers did not involve book-reading (although, of course, not all were environmental print events).

Several researchers have sought to look more closely at the use of environmental print by young children. There is, however, a difficulty involved in most of such studies. They tend to move away from naturalistic reporting as used by Payton (1984) and Lass (1982) and start to use more formal instruments to assess children's knowledge. Thus they already are beginning to move away from the genuine contextualised use of language. Kastler (1984) attempted to keep the options open by using a flexible technique. She presented a small group of kindergarteners (aged between 5 and 6 years) with a series of 21 print items. These included TV magazines, newspapers, catalogues, magazines, advertisements, library cards, credit cards, letters, etc. The children were then individually interviewed using an interview schedule that allowed considerable flexibility in probing the children's understanding of the function and use of the print material. She found that only one of the items, a library card, failed to elicit an appropriate response and she claimed that: 'Almost half the children were able to address the notion of function for each of the materials selected' (p. 94). She claimed her study demonstrated that: 'Young children are developing well formed concepts of written language prior to formal literacy instruction.'

McGee, Lomax and Head (1984) set out to describe children's efforts to read ten functional print items (newspaper, telephone book, grocery list, coupon, TV guide, letter, map, calendar, book and potato chip bag). Their sample was quite large (81 children) and the ages of the children ranged from three to six years. They deliberately chose their items to be different from those particular signs and labels with which the children would be familiar. Thus the criteria were more demanding than in many other studies. All the children were asked to identify each item and asked 'What could I read here?' and 'What can you tell me about what it might say?' Their results indicated that most of the attempts to read were meaningful and that 50% of the attempts to read consisted of single words or names and indicated some attention to graphic detail. They claim: 'Children's responses to different print items indicated an awareness of different kinds of language which are associated with different print items, as well as sensitivity to the print display and how that might influence reading responses' (p. 13), and: 'Children attend to all sorts of print that surrounds them in a highly meaningful way. Not only do they know the type of print-conveyed meaning associated with different print items performing different literacy functions, but they also are sensitive to the language cues, including graphic detail, in written language' (p. 15).

One of the most detailed reports of investigation into print awareness is that of Goodman and Altwerger (1981). They had a small sample of children from 3–5 years old and, unlike many American studies, their children came from poorer backgrounds and different racial and ethnic groups. Half their children had parents who were divorced or separated. Each child took part in six tasks of which three were print awareness tasks. Goodman and Altwerger introduced the idea of gradually decontextualising the print. In the second task each child saw the same label with its 'stylised' print and colour but stripped of all familiar pictures and designs. In the third task each label had all supporting context details (pictures, design and colour) removed and it consisted solely of the graphic unit written in manuscript form.

A number of interesting points emerged from this study. Not surprisingly the ability of the children to do the tasks increased with age. More importantly, however, the style of response changed according to the demands of the task and the age of the child. When the full context was available, children paid no attention to letters or numbers, etc. but attended to the meaning of the item. As the print became more decontextualised, i.e. in task three, letter calling and attention to graphic detail increased.

The significance of this shift is in its relationship to Goodman's more general claims about the developmental nature of emerging literacy, in particular her view of the role of environmental print knowledge in the development of literacy. Goodman (1980) identifies five 'roots of literacy' of which one is the development of print awareness in situational contexts. This 'root' is 'developing simultaneously, all of them are continuously interacting and influencing each other' (p. 4).

Goodman's principles or roots are developmental 'since children grow into and through all of them. They develop idiosyncratically, depending on each child's environment, and they overlap and become integrated'

(Goodman, 1983, p. 75). Goodman sees the development of 'print awareness in situational contexts' developing in an interrelated way with what she calls the 'development of print awareness in connected discourse', in other words understanding of book language, or more generally decontextualised print.

Support for the notion that development involves a number of elements occurring simultaneously, interrelatedly and depending upon the individual experiences of children is given strong support by Hiebert (1981) and Harste, Woodward and Burke (1984). Hiebert set out specifically to test whether development occurred as a series of sequential steps with skills and concepts emerging in distinguishable order, or whether concepts and skills developed in a unified way with advances made in all areas simultaneously. She examined 60 subjects, aged from three years to five years, using a series of tests, including standardised reading readiness tests, measures involving assessing understanding of what is involved in print, and tests of knowledge about print in the environment. A substantial statistical analysis failed to find any invariant sequence in the acquisition of skills and concepts relating to reading. Hiebert found her pre-schoolers quite knowledgeable about the processes and uses of print. Her data suggests a high degree of interrelationship between the various skills and types of knowledge tested. She concludes that: 'In the course of everyday events, children observe print in their environment and see people around them using this print for various meaningful purposes. At times adults and older children may even involve young children in the use of print and how print is used, and they acquire specific information about it as well' (p. 236). It is important to note two points about the research and its results. The first is the interrelationship between the various elements tested and the second is that at no time does Hiebert suggest that exposure to environmental print on its own turns children into readers. The above quotation implies two further points. One is that becoming literate has a social dimension; other people are involved. The second is that there is no direct simple sequence from reading environmental print to reading decontextualised print; both abilities develop alongside each other.

Harste, Woodward, and Burke (1984) and Harste, Burke, and Woodward, (1982) have a rather special stance to literacy processes in young children. This stance will be discussed in more detail in Chapter 5, but, in essence, they claim that there are 'No developmental stages to literacy but rather only experience, and with it fine tuning and continued orchestration' (p. x). Contact with environmental print was a central concern of their research which was carried out over several years with preschool children from a variety of ethnic and social backgrounds. They viewed all the children, including the youngest, as engaging in literacy processes which matched in fundamental ways those of conventionally practised literates. With regard to the use of environmental print they say: 'These young language users displayed the flexibility and confidence necessary to make individual decisions which can only come with the accumulating effects of personally significant experimental confrontations with environmental print, confrontations which were initiated on the day their mothers pulled their first diaper out of the Pampers' box, and which continued through their feedings from the well marked jars of Gerber's baby food right up to their first historic encounters with the golden arches of McDonalds. So if they read boxes more conventionally than they read books it might just be that it is not because environmental print is less complex than continuous text but because it is more familiar' (1984, p. 27). Harste, Burke and Woodward would not want to separate in process terms children's experiences with environmental print from their experiences with other areas of literate behaviour. There is no place in their account for developmental stages or sequences. They, in fact, reject the term 'emergent reading' just as they reject the terms 'readiness', 'beginning reading', and 'developmental stages'. They say: 'We have no evidence that children's psycholinguistic and sociolinguistic strategies are qualitatively different from the kinds of decisions which more experienced language users make' (p. 69).

Thus the evidence from studies by Goodman and Altwerger (1981), Hiebert (1981), Harste, Burke and Woodward (1982), Harste, Woodward and Burke (1984) and Haussler (1984 and 1985), suggests that experience with environmental print is an intrinsic part of becoming a literate language user, but that such experiences operate in conjunction with many other oral and written language experiences.

The statement would not be accepted by all researchers. Snow (1983) suggests that: 'Moving from such highly contextualised reading (which many would deny is truly reading) to relatively decontextualised reading, such as reading words in isolation or reading sentences in a book where the pictures cannot be mapped easily onto the elements within the text, involves a real transition' (p.175).

Mason (1980) acknowledges that many children know a great deal about reading before they enter school, but asks: 'Is knowledge about how to print and recognise letters and words on signs and labels related to children's later recognition of words from books and their memory of them?' (p. 205). She considers it an important question as: 'It is entirely possible that children entering school who are able to read words from cereal boxes, restroom doors, store fronts and traffic signs have an important advantage over other children in learning words and reading stories' (p. 206). She devised a series of procedures to assess levels of abilities and changes in these abilities. She suggests that her results indicate a natural hierarchy in word reading. The first level is recitation; naming and printing of letters. Then signs and labels are read, especially important or frequently seen print or conspicuous print. Then a certain amount of letter analysis is involved in identifying nouns and function words. Finally, multisyllabic words and abstract nouns are read by procedures involving fairly extensive knowledge of the relationship between sound and print. She concludes that: 'Experiences of recognising words or signs, learning the alphabet, printing and naming letters provide a background for making good guesses about how to spell short words, and how to pronounce at least the first letter of short words. This, in turn, leads children to pay even greater attention to letter sounds' (p. 221). Thus Mason sees quite a specific role for contextualised print knowledge in the development of literacy. It is hierarchically embedded in the ability to deal with more decontextualised language. Mason's work, however, derives from a view of reading that is tightly bound to word identification. Her instruments for assessing the children's abilities used mostly arbitrarily selected words. Thus the responses of the children were to an imposed set of words or activities, none of which was presented in a social context. It is therefore reasonable to ask whether this 'hierarchy' was not produced as a result of presenting children with activities which made no immediate sense to them. Thus the research represented an attempt to see how children coped with abstract presentation of print rather than (as in the case of Goodman and Altwerger, and Harste, Burke and Woodward) an attempt to look at the ways children created and used print in more rational contexts.

Environmental print provides encounters with written language. As a result of these encounters, young children learn words, as well as learning about how written language works. They learn that language is meaningful; it communicates a message. They learn that it is used by human beings for the fulfilment of many objectives. It provides a vast resource for looking at and thinking about written language. When knowledge of this resource is available side by side with the other types of knowledge being developed by young children (perhaps the 'roots' proposed by Yetta Goodman), then the emergence of literacy is greatly facilitated. It does not appear that anyone is suggesting that children will be led to the analysis of decontextualised language solely by experience with environmental print. The Goodmans, Harste, Burke, and Woodward, Hiebert, and Haussler are quite specific in their claim that the emergence of literacy is multifaceted.

It is, however, clear that the vast majority of children make some use of environmental print. From the day a child asks 'What does that say?' that child is aware that print in the environment carries a message, and it becomes possible for a child to observe other language users responding to that message. The emergence of literacy is facilitated by environmental print. The knowledge accumulated about environmental print can be used to develop understanding of other print forms and in turn they will facilitate further understanding of environmental print. Environmental print is a very important source of information about written language but it is only one form. It has a vital role in the emergence of literacy in conjunction with experience of other types of written language. This chapter began with the examination of an article by Dawson which treated the environment as having nothing to offer the emergence of literacy beyond certain sensory experiences. That is clearly a narrow perspective. The environment is replete with rich examples of written language which can be, and are, used by children to develop their understanding of the ways in which written language works.

CONTINUOUS TEXT

There is almost universal agreement that listening to stories is 'good' for children who will be, or are, learning to read. There are accounts of reading instruction which make no reference to stories (Gattegno, 1969 and Doman, 1965), but it is likely that even those writers have a sympathetic view of stories supporting entry into reading. Certainly many books written for either teachers or parents extol the virtues of story reading. 'Before children go to school the best thing parents can do is read or tell stories to their children' (Thompson, 1970, p. 79), or: 'Sitting close to you physically at reading time enables him to absorb through a kind of psychological osmosis your own understanding, humour and warmth. He will catch your love of books, your enjoyment of a good story, and your appreciation of good illustrations. Last but by no means least he will cherish the special bond between you and the child that grows from sharing books' (Gould, 1978, p. 76). What is being emphasised in this quotation is that by reading stories children can be motivated to become readers because they sense 'your enjoyment' and 'your appreciation', and that reading stories is a powerful bonding agent where parent-child relationships are concerned. This appreciation of the motivational qualities is expressed clearly by Goddard (1958): 'The children we teach will vary very much in the extent to which they are familiar with books. Part of our task in preparing the children to learn to read is to introduce them to books as things to be valued, and from which come pleasurable experiences' (p. 26).

The lobby on behalf of stories has always been a powerful and persuasive one and to judge from the institutionalisation of story-time in nursery and primary schools has been a very successful one. But what exactly is the relationship between having stories read to a child, and that child's subsequent behaviour as a reader and what is it that children learn through their early contact with books and stories? The answers to these questions are not so clear and until recently it has been rather an untested proposition that there is a positive relationship between a child hearing stories, and that child emerging as a proficient reader. Recent studies have examined those two questions and the results of several studies provide evidence of some very powerful learning about literacy on the part of young children; learning which appears to be very helpful in the emergence of an ability to be a reader of continuous and decontextualised print.

The relationship between story reading and success in reading

The major evidence for the positive nature of this relationship derives from two studies: Moon and Wells (1979) and Wells (1985). The data for both studies derives from that collected as part of the longitudinal study of children's language development carried out by the Bristol Language Development Research Programme (Wells, 1981). Moon and Wells examined a wide range of variables, and looked at the relationship between those variables which included scores on two reading tests administered at the age of seven. The children's pre-school knowledge about books and literacy correlated highly with the tests at the age of seven. Wells (1985) re-examined the original data in a more detailed way and the re-analysis revealed particularly strong relationships between listening to stories and performance on reading tests at seven. Wells claims that his 'results can be taken as providing substantial support for the particularly beneficial effect of reading stories to pre-school children' (Wells, 1985). There are a couple of points concerning this data which must be taken into account. First, the transcripts yielding the data on pre-school activities added up to only 3.6 hours of each child's pre-school life. Embedded within these 3.6 hours of transcripts (which incidentally did not include any bed-time stories) were the literacy events which were subsequently considered in relation to performance on reading tests at seven years. Data on writing incidents was excluded as it occurred so rarely (perhaps because many writing activities are completed in silence), a finding dissonant with American researchers who have looked at literacy events in homes (see Chapter 4). Thus the data used was certainly restricted. Secondly, those pre-school activities were correlated with performance on reading tests which were (a) somewhat narrow in that they were conventional tests of word and sentence recognition, and (b) carried out in a structured test situation, two factors which place some restraint on a too-ready acceptance of the claim about a major relationship. Testing is, for children, a rather decontextualised activity, and the relationship could in part be between listening to stories and performing on tests. Either way a powerful relationship between listening to stories and success in school is claimed.

There are two aspects of learning literacy on which I wish to concentrate in this section. They are 'learning about what readers do' and 'learning about how text works'. Children, of course, learn other things, for instance notions about the value and status of reading as an activity, but the two areas selected for this section have a special importance for developing literacy.

Learning about what readers do

Reading is a peculiar activity. On the one hand it is often a very concrete process: we see people staring at books and newspapers, or we see them putting on their glasses to read, and we often hear them say out loud what it is that they are reading. On the other hand the complex cognitive processes which go on in readers' minds are unseen and at best can only be inferred. A newspaper may, however, also be used for wrapping and a book for pressing or supporting. As the evidence available to young children is both visible and invisible and sometimes rather variable, so inferences made are inevitably going to vary. When I asked my niece at the age of 2½ what her mother was doing, she replied: 'Nothing, she's just looking at the paper.' Looking at the paper had not been noted as an activity worthy of the designation 'reading'. Reading was something that belonged to a particular type of activity involving herself, her parents and books.

Relying on visual evidence can have amusing consequences which appear at first sight to be evidence of confusion. It is, however, perfectly clear that, given the evidence available to children, their conclusions are quite reasonable. I have for some time been asking pre-school and reception class children whether animals can read and write. Some of my students returned from an interview session reporting that: 'Animals can't read because cats go miaow and dogs go bow wow.' The children perceived reading as an oral activity. Accompanying this is often the belief that dogs and cats (or other animals) cannot read because they don't have hands. A similar report was made by Scollon and Scollon (1981, p. 62): 'Rachel was trying to get her mother to read to her. Her mother told her to read it herself. Rachel asked, "How can I read?" Her mother said, "With your eyes." She answered, "I can't hold books with my eyes." ' In later discussion Rachel claimed that her baby brother could not read: 'Because his hands were too small but would be able to when his hands grew. The dog, though, would never be able to read because he had no hands' (p. 62). I have found that children believe that parrots could learn to read, and monkeys, possessing hands, could learn to write, but it is not until five to seven years that children start saying that animals cannot read because 'they are not human', or 'they haven't got brains'. The idea that reading is a distinctly human activity or that it involves inner mental processing appears to be a much later development and may be due in part to instruction and an increasing metacognitive ability. The point of these examples is that children are attempting to make sense of the activity of being a reader in ways that are clearly sensible. In order to form their views the children need evidence and evidence is what can be supplied in abundance by participation in story telling.

As parents read stories with children they often engage in activities which provide children with information about what it is that readers do. Children also make statements and ask questions to which adults respond. As a result of these experiences they can become aware of what readers do and how print functions. They may, for example, observe that:

- when we read we rely on the print to carry the message;

- we read and use books in a particular order – from front to back;

- we follow the print in a certain order: line by line, word by word;

- books and print have a certain orientation;

- print is made up of letters, words, punctuation and spaces;
- there are relationships between the words spoken and the print observed;
- print is different from pictures;
- there is a language associated with the activity of reading books: front, back, page, word, letter, etc.

All these, and others, are not self-evident concepts although experienced readers may consider them so. Children have to learn them. Not all children will have the experiences necessary for them to infer all the points listed above. As a result of the work of Clay (1979c) and Downing (1979) far more teachers in nursery and infant schools are helping children to learn about these points, not by direct instruction but through discussion and demonstration during story-time. The evidence relating to the extent to which children do understand those concepts seems contradictory. Both Clay (1979) and Downing (1979) are interested in this area precisely because their research tends to show that children have only weak, and often incorrect, understandings of those concepts. On the other hand Goodman (1983) suggests that those results occur as a consequence of subjecting children to formal testing situations. She points out that children can often do, in context, what they fail to reveal in a formal test: 'For example, part of the task we have given our readers is book handling. I hold up a page in a book, wave it back and forth and say, "What is this?" None of the 12 three and four year olds I did this with last could answer the question. However, as I read them a story and came to the end of the print on the page I'd say, "What should I do now?" Everyone of the children I asked replied, "Turn the page."' (Goodman, 1983, p. 73). Some of the reasons for these different results are explored in Chapter 5.

One final point worth considering is the extent to which children understand that people write books. Understanding this may not help them to become readers but it could help them to become writers. Authorship is a complex idea when one is faced solely by a glossy, printed product. Crago and Crago (1983) made a special point of helping their child Anna learn that 'books were the creation of individual human beings. We would customarily point to photographs of author or artist on the jacket of the volume and explain that this was the person "who made this book". We made a practice of reading the text of all title pages, with their ascription of authorship' (p. 238). It is too easy for children to believe that books have some kind of mystical existence, or that they are the product of bookshops. Many children nowadays think that milk derives solely from bottles, or seeds solely from packets. Children may see the writing and reading of stories as a more reasonable activity if they understand it to be a distinctly human activity.

Learning about how text works

This is perhaps the most important understanding to be derived from hearing stories read aloud. It is in the nature of continuous text that it is usually considerably more decontextualised than the print on signs and notices. In other words, the meanings have to be assigned to the text. There are fewer aspects of context to support the assigning of meaning and they are often different from the contextual clues on environmental print. Such clues as exist are, however, of exceptional importance. A beginning reader is able to draw on his linguistic knowledge of how oral language works, but how much more useful it is if a child can also draw on a knowledge of how written language works. A child who has an intimate knowledge of written language styles and conventions will find written language more predictable. Being able to 'talk like a book' (Clay, 1979c) may be of critical value in becoming a complete reader. Clay uses the term 'talk like a book' in a wider sense than that implied in this section. She includes in her definition an element referred to as 'a special type of talking', where the child learns to use the type of talk found in books.

Aspects of this special kind of talk may be evident at a very young age. Scollon and Scollon (1981) point out that such 'talk' is not a universal phenomenon but a cultural one. Sometimes we need to contrast our own assumptions with those of another social group to make us aware that they are cultural assumptions and not absolute ways of doing things. Such an opportunity was provided for the Scollons when they worked in Alberta, Alaska. They had with them their two year old daughter. As a result of comparing their daughter's behaviour with that of the children in the native community, the Scollons came to the conclusion that: 'Rachel was in most ways literate before she learned to read, that for her learning to read was little more than learning spelling conventions because of the systematic preparation in the literate orientation that we had given her' (p. 61). They claim that by the age of two years Rachel had achieved, in respect of literacy: 'a typification of a set of activities and behaviours, a distribution amongst social roles, and a set of values and attitudes that corresponded to ours' (p. 64). For the children in the native community: 'Literacy was inappropriate. For adults it was unidirectional, one read but did not write. Literacy was socially located, not in the home but in the church and subsidiarily in the school' (p. 64). The Scollons claimed that their daughter's incipient ability to use literacy was rooted in the 'fictionalisation of self'; a characteristic of what they call 'essayist literacy', the type of literacy which pervades much (but not all) Western literate culture, in particular schooling. Stories were a primary mechanism by which Rachel came to fictionalise herself: 'For her literacy was a natural part of the home, and one of the good things at that. She asked much more often to be read stories than to be given special foods' (p. 62). This ability to fictionalise self meant that even in Rachel's relatively simple stories (some of which she 'wrote' down) there was clear evidence of the inclusion of essayist devices such as: 'Once upon a time there was'.

(There are many more subtler examples than these drawn out in the Scollons' analysis on pp. 76–9 of their book.) The native children on the other hand, even when much older (aged 10), when attempting to act out a story for writing down, created their stories in a form characteristic of face-to-face oral performance.

Rachel's emerging literacy was powerfully clear. She was able to tell a story about herself from a third person stance, i.e. she could see herself as an author. She knew how to focus on a book rather than herself. She could play around with her own activities and language in order to 'talk like a book'. She was able to act as commentator on aspects of her world. She drew extensively on written sources and could create stories that began to demonstrate her use of literary convention and style. Once she commented while watching her father chop an onion: 'Chuck, chuck, chuck. That's what the knife said to the onion' (p. 91). The freedom of movement of these characters and the literary stance towards the episode are characteristic of the decontextualised style of story books. Rachel did not believe she had been taught such skills. When she was asked 'Who taught you to write stories?' she replied, 'Nobody, I learned it myself.'

Understanding and using narrative book-like skills depends both on development and experience, the experience being exposure to stories read aloud. These stories will present children with access to a variety of styles of written language use, access to conventions involved in talking like a book, and access to a way of using language that depends for its effect on the manipulation of language rather than context. Such experiences will contain many surprises for young learners, but it is the child's resolution of the problems implicit within these surprises which constitutes the learning. Anna (aged three years and two months), the daughter of Crago and Crago (1983) was certainly surprised during a story by Beatrix Potter. After a story composed mainly in the third person, Potter concluded with: 'And I think that some day I shall have to make another larger book to tell you about Tom Kitten.' Anna swiftly commented: 'Who said that?'. It was not until Anna was four years and eight months that her parents collected evidence of her understanding and acceptance of these shifts in the writer's stance.

By the time children are five the complexity of their own narratives is considerable. Fox (1983) investigated the narrative competence in the story monologues of a group of children aged three and a half to six years. She provides some very rich examples, including one from Julie (aged five), the beginning of which (including Fox's analysis) is reproduced below:

Hello, I'm Jill	Narrator as broadcaster
I'm going to tell you a st . . . another story about a boy this time	Narrator as communicator to audience
A boy called Cletcher	Narrator as director of narrative (subject matter)

A very funny name	Narrator as evaluator
I made it up	Narrator as communicator to audience and director of narrative
Cletcher was a good boy	Narrator as storyteller
His mother and father said he could go to the fair one day	Narrator as director of dialogue using narratised speech

(Fox, 1983, p. 17)

Book reading is a significant contributor to this richness of stylistic structure. Fox (1985) found that for some of the children studied, books were used much more often than personal experience. One child drew on more than forty books in constructing 86 monologues. She identifies three levels of use of books (Fox, 1985):

1 At a minimal or superficial level: the name of a character from a book, a small part of plot, the quotation of a phrase or sentence.

2 At the level of linguistic style: quotations or near quotations sometimes make the source of the language style identifiable but normally stylistic influence operates in a more subtle and diffuse way; the language sounds unlike ordinary five year old speech and more like that of books.

3 At the level of larger techniques and forms which are found in books which the children have heard and transformed by them to their own story-telling purposes.

Her study clearly shows that children acquire a high level of understanding of complex narrative rules as a result of their experiences with books. The level of ability achieved is frequently above that of the reading scheme texts which children meet in school. As Fox says: 'The majority of such books come nowhere near using the many narrative conventions children can learn just by listening to good stories read aloud; and they are even further away from the literary competencies the children are acquiring' (Fox, 1983, p.24).

Wells (1985) makes the point that it is stories in books, not just books, which influence future ability to perform in school settings. He rates picture books (although it is not totally clear how he defines picture books) as less effective because their use is frequently limited to straightforward labelling interactions. It is not that these interactions are unimportant, but they do not acquaint children with the decontextualised aspects of texts. Wells says that successful participation in school requires specific types of language use. These language uses consist of being able to use language and thinking to analyse language and thinking, and being able to interpret and evaluate different ways in which language is used. Ultimately this means the manipulation of symbols in a totally decontextualized way; language being used solely to explore ideas. Wells sees this language use as intimately related to written language. Stories 'provide the child with the opportunity to discover the power that language has to create and explore alternative possible worlds with their own inner coherence and logic' (p.251). Wells feels that books need to be introduced to children at an early age because, with experience of decontextualised language, they will be better equipped to participate in curricular-related talk at school. He is insistent though that it is not the story itself but the interaction between parent and child which is important. 'If stories are simply read as part of a daily routine, without being discussed, they are likely to remain inert and without much impact on the rest of the child's experience. If they are used chiefly as the basis for display question sequences that focus on the meanings of particular words or isolated items, such as the names of characters or the details of particular events, again they are unlikely to provide encouragement for the exploratory but controlled thinking that written language facilitates' (p.253).

The kind of school environment that Wells has in mind has been seen as parallel to the experience of children from 'mainstream' families (Heath, 1982). Such schools may well be seen as a product of particular social groups. Thus values, attitudes and beliefs about education are shared by both school and mainstream communities. The work of Heath (1982 and 1983) demonstrates clearly that even within a Western, literacy-oriented culture there are many other ways of thinking about literacy and that stories may well fulfil other functions in these communities. In particular her work demonstrates 'what no bedtime story means' (Heath, 1982).

In the mainstream home, children are exposed to literacy behaviours related to books at a very early age.

- As early as six months children give attention to books and information from books.
- From six months children acknowledge questions about books.
- Children respond to conversational allusions to the content of books and behave as if they possess a knowledge of books.
- After two years of age children use their knowledge of what books are to legitimise their departures from the 'truth'.
- Young children accept books and related activities as entertainment.
- Young children announce their own factual and fictional narratives.
- After children reach three years of age adults tend to discourage interactive participation roles in book-reading and children learn to listen and wait as an audience.

The above elements, drawn from Heath (1982), characterise the authority which books and book-related behaviour have in the lives of mainstream children. Children in those homes have, by the time they enter school 'developed habits of performing which enable them to run through the hierarchy of preferred knowledge about literacy and the appropriate sequence of skills to be displayed in showing knowledge of a subject. They have developed ways of decontextualising and surrounding with explanatory prose the knowledge gained from selective attention to objects' (p.56). In nursery schools they continue to develop these skills (Cochran-Smith, 1984), learning to listen and wait for appropriate cues. In short, claims Heath, those children have developed:

1 all those habits associated with 'what' explanations;
2 selective attention to items of written text;
3 appropriate interactional styles for orally displaying all the know-
    how of their literate orientation to the environment. (Heath, 1983,
    p.56)

Such is the experience of most of the children in the research already cited in this chapter. Heath, however, also looks at two other communities: 'Roadville', a white working-class community and 'Trackton', a black working-class community. In both communities children went to school with certain expectations and a certain level of competence with print as a result of their pre-school experiences. There were, however, considerable differences in the role of stories in their lives and these differences had consequences for the children's ability to fit into, and benefit from, a mainstream educational system.

The Roadville children grow up in a community which values literacy and they have books as possessions. Reading activities occur most frequently at bed-time, but in Roadville book-reading tends to focus on letters of the alphabet, numbers, names of items, and simplified retelling by the adult. Adults do not relate incidents or objects in stories to the world outside books. 'Children are not encouraged to move their understanding of books into other situational contexts or to apply it in their general knowledge of the world about them' (p.61). The emphasis in book experience at later stages is on practising doing things correctly because that is the convention. Roadville adults do not encourage literacy activities beyond book-readings. Roadville children do not fictionalise themselves in stories about the world and its events, as Rachel Scollon did with her story about the onion and the knife, because in Roadville any fictionalised account of a real event is seen as a lie. Thus children do not get support or experience in decontextualising their knowledge. These children get the equivalent of picture book reading which according to Wells is a less important use of a story where future school success is concerned.

When Roadville children go to school initially they do well. They are good at labellings and simple skill activities involving relatively routine and undemanding tasks. When they progress through school and the demand shifts to activities requiring more advanced and independent thinking then Roadville children cease to progress. Heath says: 'As the importance and frequency of questions and reading habits with which they are familiar decline in the higher grades, they have no way of keeping up or of seeking help in learning what it is they do not even know they don't know' (p.64).

Trackton children experience an almost non-book environment. From birth the children are centred in the world of oral communication. Their toys are trucks, balls, dolls, etc., hardly ever puzzles or books. There are no reading materials for children, and adults do not sit and read to children. Only occasionally do older children read to younger ones but it is usually as part of a play activity. Children are asked mainly analogical questions; a question will ask for open-ended comparisons between objects or events – 'What's that like?' The adults do not simplify language, label items or features. Instead: 'Children are continually contextualised, presented with almost continuous communication. From this ongoing, multiple-channelled stream of stimuli, they must themselves select, practice, and determine rules of production and structuring' (p.68). When these children arrive at school they are asked to engage in specific naming tasks and label detailed, pre-selected features. Their performance on tests is usually low and not only do they fail to learn the content of lessons but they also do not adopt the social interactional rules for school literacy events. The children's skills in analogic reasoning are not tapped by these activities and this may indeed cause difficulties. By the time they reach levels where such skills are valued (they are usually seen as higher order skills) these children have, in effect, opted out.

What causes both Trackton and Roadville children difficulty is lack of experience in using alternative ways of learning. Their strategies for coping with different environments are limited. The mainstream children, with their facility to work in a decontextualised way have an advantage in conventional schooling as they have had the chance to 'come to grips with the symbolic potential of language – its power to represent experience in symbols independent of the objects, events, and relationships which are symbolised, and which can be interpreted in contexts other than those in which the experience originally occurred' (Wells, 1982, p.147) and according to Wells 'stories read aloud and discussed in a way which encourages reflection upon their own experience and imaginative exploration of the world created through the language of text are probably the best way of helping young children to begin to develop these abilities' (Wells, 1982, p.154).

Such an approach towards stories and schoolings may make it appear as if yet another facet of a cultural deficit model has been introduced. In fact what Heath is pointing out is that literacy does not emerge in all children in the same way, yet almost all research has been carried out within the confines of the mainstream view of education and culture. There are other ways of acquiring communicative competence, and therefore assumptions about how children emerge as literate will have to be based on wider knowledge than is currently available. The essayist tradition of mainstream culture is not self-evidently the best possible: Postman (1970) has pointed out some of its defects but perhaps we are so used to our own conception of literacy that we have forgotten to explore beyond it and are incapable of recognising that it may have limitations. Street (1984) has suggested an alternative view which 'treats sceptically claims by Western liberal educators for the "openness", "rationality", and critical awareness of what they teach' (p. 2). Or as Scollon and Scollon (1982) put it: 'We can no longer assume that essayist literacy should be the goal of all education any more than we should assume that all schoolchildren should be ethnically identified with any one dominant group' (p. 98).

CONCLUSION

The emphasis in this chapter on the importance of stories for emerging literacy should not hide the fact that stories are not an absolute necessity for a child to become literate. Torrey (1969) tells of a child who learned to read almost solely from looking at advertisements on television. Both Clark (1976) and Durkin (1966) found early readers who had few or no stories read to them, and Teale (1984) reports that he found a number of children who had not been read to during their early years who were nevertheless above-average achievers in reading at school. Thus the message would seem to be that although stories can have a powerful and valuable impact on emerging literacy the combination of a whole range of written language experiences, of which stories should be a part, is more likely to optimise the emergence of literacy.

4 The emergent writer

INTRODUCTION

Writing is often a more visible activity than reading. In spite of writing's 'visibility' the myth persists that children do not know anything about writing until they are taught it at school. The conventional assumptions outlined in Chapter 1 apply as much to the teaching of writing as they do to the teaching of reading. In 1983 I collected a piece of paper given out by a Local Education Authority to explain to parents and other interested adults ideas about children being taught to write. The leaflet states: 'Unlike talking, writing does not occur naturally to most people and before writing, one has to learn how to. Young children learn to form writing patterns, then form letters and from them words and sentences.' It goes on: 'Children learn to form sentences, to spell, to punctuate, to form paragraphs, to write stories, reports, accounts of experiments, letters and so on.'

Those two sentences contain most of the assumptions outlined in Chapter 1. Writing does not occur naturally – it must therefore be taught. It must be taught through a sequence beginning with handwriting patterns. It is composed of a set of skills: letter formation and so on. The emphasis is quite clearly on handwriting and structure as opposed to authorship and conveying meanings. Forming sentences, spelling and punctuation came, in the quoted sentence, before writing stories and other more meaningful writing. A later sentence illustrates this clearly: 'Writing is one of the slowest forms of communication not only because of the restraint imposed by having to learn how to do handwriting (or typing) first but also because of the requirements of grammar, spelling, vocabulary as well as punctuation; all of which have to be learnt.' There is not the slightest suggestion that writing might be a slow process because composing meaningful messages demands reflective authorship. Authorship is a kind of afterthought according to this document. Authorship is slow because handwriting is slow, because one has to take into account punctuation, spelling, vocabulary and grammar. Of course, such things are part and parcel of the total proficiency involved in the effective communication of messages, but they are only a part. The lack of balance reflected in this LEA handout is typical of the emphasis placed upon certain aspects of teaching writing in schools. Bennett, Desforges, Cockburn and Wilkinson (1984) when examining the teaching of writing in infant classes found that: 'Requests for spellings constitute the predominant teacher/pupil exchanges in language lessons' (p. 128), and that 'The predominant aim expressed in more than 70% of tasks intended to promote writing was to "practise writing" and to use some aspects of grammar, especially capital letters and full stops as sentence markers' (p. 101).

Wells (1985) seems to sum up such a typical approach to the teaching of literacy: 'The result is that children in many classrooms – and even in some homes – spend long hours in repetitive and routine activities involving simple pictorial representations and geometrical shapes' (p. 249). He does not deny that being able to decode new words or being able to spell conventionally is important: 'But to focus on them to the near exclusion of the content and purpose of written communications, and the mode of thinking that these characteristically involve, is to stunt the development of literacy rather than to promote it.'

The emergence of writing has received far less exposure than the emergence of reading. No one has written books to match those studies of early readers. There have been no books on 'Young fluent writers' or 'Children who write early'. The reason is no doubt partly historical; reading seemed to demand all the research. If the articles and books published this century on reading were balanced against those on writing, the scales would crash down under the weight of articles on reading. It is only relatively recently that research has rediscovered writing and the imbalance is being redressed. Perhaps part of the reason for this upsurge in investigations into writing was the realisation that most adults do not actually like writing and so avoid it whenever possible. As Graves (1978) put it: 'Writing is extolled over, worried over, cited as a national priority, but seldom practised' (p. 636). It is something of a paradox that children spend more time on writing at school than on any other activity, yet it is writing that is rejected as soon as children leave school. Is there a relationship? The revival of interest in writing was accompanied by the use of more naturalistic observation, the result of which has been to demonstrate clearly that nearly all young children are emergent writers. They almost all know something about the nature and purpose of writing; knowledge which is too often rejected by schools and replaced by exercises with no purpose other than the practice of almost totally decontextualised skills.

Some researchers have found little evidence of early writing in homes. Wells's study on the relationship between home and school did contain a category called 'writing or pretending to write'. He comments: 'The last category occurred so rarely that it subsequently had to be omitted from the analysis' (Wells, 1985, p. 145). Heath also found that in mainstream homes: 'Writing was less acceptable as an "anytime" activity, since adults have rigid rules about times, places and materials for writing' (Heath, 1982, p. 53). In Roadville homes, opportunities for children writing were: 'Largely forced by others – parents forcing them to write thank you notes, teachers giving assignments and coaches asking them to sign pledges of good behaviour' (Heath, 1983, p. 218). Those children were of school age. At the pre-school age it was also a forced task. 'They are given workbooks, and encouraged to write their names, draw straight lines, color in the lines, follow the numbers' (Heath, 1983, p. 228). In Trackton homes there were few opportunities for writing but Heath nevertheless found that Gary (aged four years and six months) when representing a newspaper knew that the letters in headlines were larger than those in the text, and that the lines of text were organised horizontally. Mel (aged four) 'pretend' wrote a letter which included an identifiable date, salutation, text, closure and signature. The children's experience was very much self-initiated and restricted to highly contextualised forms. In the community: 'There are few occasions for reading of extended connected discourse and almost no occasions for writing such material' (Heath, 1983, p. 198). Thus writing does not seem to have been a frequently practised activity by those children.

It is possible that pre-school writing may simply have been missed in those two studies. This is more likely to have been the case in the Wells study than in Heath's study, not because the Wells study was poorly designed but because it was not designed to collect such evidence. It was designed to collect 'talk' rather than writing. The methods of data collection could easily have led to writing experiences being overlooked. This possibility is reinforced by Taylor's work on family literacy. She wrote: 'Many of the children's writing activities pass unnoticed as the children's momentary engagement merges with the procession of other interests' and 'Even when I showed the mothers the scraps of paper collected from their homes, they were uncertain as to whom they belonged or, for that matter, when they had been produced' (Taylor, 1983, p. 56). She cites as an example of this: 'Moving around the kitchen while we talked, I picked up a piece of yellow lined paper off a counter top. I asked Jill if it was for my collection. She looked at it and said, "No, I don't know where that came from." Steven (aged four) walked into the kitchen and I asked him if he knew anything about the paper. He said, "Sure, I just did it." While we were talking Steven was drawing letters. No one was watching him and no one had seen him put the paper on the counter top – perfect example of unnoticed momentary writing activities' (p. 58). The children that Taylor studied were 'mainstream' children who may anyway know more than they are sometimes allowed to reveal. Hall et al. (1986) looked at a nursery class which was conventionally set out but in which writing was an exceptional event. There was a lot of painting and making but it was seldom that the children incorporated writing into those activities or any of their other play activities. It would have been easy to characterise those children as having little interest in, and knowledge of, writing. The authors of the study changed the non-literate home corner into a 'literate' home corner. Various kinds of writing utensils and materials for writing were added. Equipment had appropriate literacy materials placed nearby, for instance the telephone had directories, notepads, pens and pencils near to it. (It is important to note that appropriate writing instruments were offered to the children; how many adults write in crayon? Both Baghban (1984) and Harste, Woodward and Burke (1984) found that children responded to the type of instruments they considered appropriate and would not write if the 'wrong' instruments were given to them.) The effects of these changes to the home corner were dramatic. Children filled hundreds of sheets of paper with writing. They sent letters, and filled notebooks, diaries and calendars. They took messages, created restaurants and took orders. They also engaged in a lot of reading behaviours. Those children when offered the chance to write demonstrated a high degree of commitment to writing, an understanding of when and why people wrote, and they demonstrated, to varying degrees, levels of conventional writing performance.

Many investigations of recent years have found a great deal of evidence about emergent writing abilities. Some have looked at individual children at home (Bissex, 1980; Baghban, 1984; and Kammler, 1984); others have looked beyond single children at home (Read, 1970; Heath, 1983; and Gundlach et al., 1985) while others have looked at emergent writers in nursery and kindergarten settings (Ferreiro and Teberosky, 1983; Harste, Burke and Woodward, 1982, and 1984; Sulzby, 1985 and Dyson, 1985). Rather than looking at these studies one by one, it will be more helpful to consider contributions in the context of the three areas noted by Hall et al. (1986). To what extent do these contributions answer the questions: 'Do young children have a commitment to writing?'; 'Do they understand anything about when and why people write?'; 'To what extent do they know about how people write?'

Do young children have a commitment to writing?

Writing has its origins both in the making of marks and the communication of meaning. The duality is evident not only in the origins of writing but also in the way writing is taught in school where the claim is that both are important, although the bulk of practice is given to the making of marks. Gibson (1970) reports that a child aged 12 months will make marks on paper if given materials. At 14 months a child can make a definite scribble in 'progressive, continuous tracing' (Gibson, 1970, p. 136). By 18 months a child will initiate scribbling on its own and at 30 months a child can draw a line as distinct from a circle. Gibson and Yonas (cit. in Gibson, 1970) found that children soon ceased to make marks if the marker did not leave a trace. Making marks was an enjoyable experience for children who 'were eager for the experimentor to look at them and demanded that she did so' (Gibson, 1970, p. 137). At some point in a child's development differentiation occurs and scribbling is separated from drawing, and writing from both of them, but for some children certain elements of the distinctive properties of these three mark-making systems are learned easily.

Baghban (1984) gives an extensive, clearly written and illustrated account of her daughter's emergent writing over a period from birth to three. Reading of the account leaves the reader in no doubt that Giti (the child) grew up in a mainstream family where there was considerable support from an environment extremely rich in literacy events. However, it is important to consider this example not as a case of a very bright child, or of very bright parents, or of parents with a specific interest in literacy, but as an example of a child interacting with certain kinds of print experiences. As Harste, Burke and Woodward (1984) suggest, intellect and development may be less important than experience.

Giti frequently saw her parents write. Telephone messages were taken, grocery lists written, thank you notes and cards were sent, cheques were filled in, forms completed, and academic work continued. Prior to 17 months Giti would come and observe the activity. At 17 months she would grab pens and paper and 'scribble'. Her parents filled a drawer with paper for her to use and provided pens. Giti's mother even carried a notebook for Giti to use while in restaurants or waiting for appointments. It is interesting to note that Giti was reluctant to use crayons; she would prefer to use ballpoint or felt-tipped pens. Giti's grandparents visited and drew rather than wrote with her. 'By 19 months her scribbling did not sprawl over the page to such an extent, and she appeared to have noticed dots in other's writings' (p. 47). Giti would write frequently after having seen an adult write and in those circumstances her productions more closely resembled English script than did her independent creations. Those demonstrations seemed powerful sources of data for understanding the nature of writing. At 21 months she 'wrote' over print, i.e. on newspapers and circulars. When she was asked to write she made circles. On occasions when asked to write she gave a word. 'When asked "What did you draw?" she did not respond' (p. 51). At 23 months her writing sessions lasted on average about ten minutes and she began to use her book babbling oral language in her own writing. At 24 months she attemped an 'M' in her writing. This coincided with her beginning to read certain environmental signs; a clue to the importance of interrelationships of experience in the emergence of literacy. At 25 months Giti would practise Gs. At 26 months her parents bought her a desk and she was able to keep all her writing materials together. Giti at this age did not always distinguish between drawing and writing in her own productions, but consistently asked her grandparents to 'draw' for her, and her parents 'to write' for her. At 27 months Giti would dictate to her parents and demand they wrote. Some of these sessions lasted 20 minutes. On her own she began to compose letters, and was writing some of the letters from her own name. At 28 months after a meal in a restaurant Giti 'took a small pad from the telephone stand and a pencil, stood in front of me with the pencil poised over the pad ... and said, "You want?"' (p. 61). Entries were made in the pad and the game continued for 20 minutes: another example of the impact of demonstrations (and similar demonstrations were used to great effect by Booth and Hall, 1986, in helping deaf children to appreciate the nature and purpose of literacy). At the same age Giti reproduced a good version of a calendar seen in a neighbour's house. Although she did not write numbers as such 'she sang 2, 9, 6, 4, 3 while writing, which demonstrated that she had indeed noticed the numbers in the boxes on the calendar' (p. 63). By 29 months her dictations were frequently as long as 25 words and could last half an hour. At this age: 'While she continued to confuse writing and drawing on her oral language, an adult observer could note differences' (p. 66). At 30 months she independently wrote her own name. By 32 months she was clearly distinguishing writing from drawing. At this time her writing began to go from right to left and from top to bottom, and her letter-writing and mailing took up a lot of her writing time. In her 34th month her writing went from left to right and returned from the edge of the paper and she sometimes underlined.

This account, which should be read and seen in the original for the full flavour of Giti's development, ceases at age three. At this age Giti was 'writing' with correct orientation, returning to the beginning of the line and moving down the page. She distinguished between drawing and writing (sometimes representing both clearly on one sheet of paper). She understood clearly that writing conveyed messages and that writing was composed of smaller bits which were sometimes letters or numbers. Giti was not exceptional. Harste, Burke and Woodward (1984) claimed in their study: 'We have found that by the age of three all children in our study could under certain conditions, distinguish art from writing' (p. 18) and they show in an example the consistency with which these three year olds represented their names across sessions. Harste, Burke and Woodward caution: 'Lest we forget, these are the writings of lower and middle-class black and white children, not of the upper class children who supposedly have some school literacy advantages' (p. 18). The authors claim that the productions of those three year olds 'are not pseudo-preliterate marks or acts but, both in form and process, the stuff of real literacy, being invented from the inside out' (p. 18). Harste, Burke and Woodward (1984) and Hall et al. (1986) found no reluctance whatsoever on the part of the children to use written language. Certainly none of the studies of individual children have found any reluctance to write. Most authors collected hundreds of sheets of paper. Hall et al. (1986) found that when presented by an adult with the question: 'Can you write?' many children said no. However, when faced with appropriate materials, in an appropriate setting, they had no hesitation in using the materials to write in meaningful ways. Neither Giti, the children in the Harste, Burke and Woodward study, nor those in the Hall et al. study lacked any commitment to write. This commitment is what enables Graves (1983) to say: 'Children want to write. They want to write the first day they attend school' (p. 3).

Do children know when and why people write?

'At age four, Shaun changed his name to Ponch, asked for a black wig and began playing CHIPS(California Highway Patrol). This involved zooming around on his two wheeler with a pencil and pad tucked in his back pocket. Like his macho, motor cycle riding TV hero, my son, Ponch, issued hundreds of tickets to the law abiding citizens of Wagga over the next few years' (Kammler, 1984, p. 61).

Fortunately for emergent literates there are many examples of written language use which are not difficult to understand, providing one can contextualise the situation. If Ponch had no idea about policing, parking, speeding offences and rules of law in his country then the activity of issuing tickets would make little sense. Ponch, however, knew more than just the context; he knew about the function of the literacy event known as giving a ticket. Clearly he also knew more than that. 'While Ponch was more concerned with the activity of ticket giving than with how the ticket should be written, the form of his writing is never random or disorganised. Left to right directionality, linearity, uniformity of size and shape and growing control of the letters of the alphabet are evident in the tickets' (p. 63). As Kammler points out, playing this game put Shaun in touch with one way adults in his culture use writing.

Bissex reports about her son: Five-year-old Paul was in the house. I was outside on the deck reading. After he had tried unsatisfactorily to talk with me, he decided to get my attention a new way – to break through print with print. Selecting the rubber letter stamps he needed from his set, Paul printed and delivered this message: RUDF (Are you deaf?). Of course I put down my book' (Bissex, 1980, p. 3). Paul was a prolific writer and inventor of spellings, but he often wrote to some purpose. He could use writing to make declarations: DO NOT DSTRB GNYS AT WRK (Do not disturb. Genius at work); he could use writing to indicate prohibitions: DO NAT KM.IN.ANE.MOR.JST.LETL.KES (Do not come in any more. Just little kids); and he could use writing to signify achievement: THA.BEG.EST HOS.EN.THA.WRALD (The biggest house in the world). Paul's earliest writings were used to convey feelings. They were not written for experimentation but to communicate. He wrote: 'the banner to welcome me home from a trip, the strings of letters typed as notes to friends, and the page of green letters to make me feel better' (Bissex, 1980. p. 6). Paul was clearly capable by the age of five of understanding many of the subtle ways of using writing.

The range of purposes understood by children may well be less than those used by some adults (Goodman, 1980), but it still represents a wide spectrum of events. Many interesting uses of writing show up in a study of pre-schoolers by Schickedanz (1984). There was a child who wanted to act as secretary at meetings: 'She asked me to sharpen her new multicoloured pencils. I did. She then wrote various things on her steno pad. That's the one I got her to take to the meetings where I take notes. She had to have one too, you know' (p. 12); there was the child who kept a diary: 'Then she asked me for help with her diary. She wanted to make one. Like Martha's in the George and Martha story. So I did help her. I got a notebook and she could write things in it and it's secret. It was her writing in it, that scribble kind of writing' (p. 12); there was the child who kept a calendar: 'Thursday she marked days on her calendar for when grandma and poppa would come and visit. She makes the calendar each month with her dad. They draw the lines and she fills the numbers in' (p. 13); the child who made the grocery list: 'In the morning M wrote out a grocery list with me. She asked me how to spell out some of the words. Then later we went to the grocery stores and she took her list with her' (p. 16); and the child who functioned as a reporter: 'She got a pencil and she said to my father, "What do you do all day?" And he said, "I play golf." So she said, "Golf. How do you spell that?" He spelled it for her. Then she said, "How do you do it?" It was like an interview. I don't know where she ever saw this, whether it was like on *Electric Company* [television programme], or what' (p. 17).

Add to this list greetings cards, thank you cards, lists to Father Christmas, letters, menus, waiters' notepads and even stories, and it is possible to see that children are exposed to a range of writing events whose purposes are quite clear, and which in their breadth, help children understand the purposes of written communication. There is little doubt that many children are familiar with the 'when' and 'why' of written communication, and the emergence of these understandings plays a central role in contextualising the whole activity of being 'instructed' in reading and writing in school. Whether all children are as familiar as the mainly 'mainstream' children in the studies cited here is not so clear. The Roadville and Trackton children of Heath's study certainly did not seem to have access to quite the same range of writing events as the 'mainstream' children. However, the children in the Hall *et al.* (1986) study came from a wide variety of backgrounds and few avoided the chance to create written language; between them they managed to explore an extremely wide range of written language functions.

Do children know how people write?

There are two aspects to this question. One relates to what could be called the physical properties of writing and the other relates to the use of elements of written language to compose particular messages, in other words the use of the alphabetic nature of English language. This section will give brief attention to both these aspects.

As we have already seen, even very young children are aware that the marks that constitute writing have certain physical characteristics. Giti (Baghban, 1984) distinguished between writing and drawing and Harste, Woodward and Burke (1984) claimed that under certain circumstances all their children could distinguish between writing and art. A quite extraordinary demonstration of sensitivity to the form of writing was observed by Harste, Burke and Woodward (1982). They asked a group of four year old children in a multi-ethnic class to 'write everything you can write'. The scribble 'writing' of the white American girl looked quite different from the scribble 'writing' of the Saudi Arabian girl, who said: 'You can't read it, it's in Arabic.' Both sets of 'writing' were different from that of an Israeli child.

This sensitivity to the kind of marks people make when they write is considered in the writing principles selected by Clay (1975). Clay identifies thirteen 'principles' which relate more to an exploration of mark-making than to an analysis of alphabetic language. These principles which, Clay claims, may be observed in the writing behaviour of young children, are not in any particular order:

1 The sign concept
A sign carries a message but the sign is complete in itself and not related to a way of representing alphabetically the name signified by the sign.

2 The message concept
The child understands that messages can be written down but there is no correspondence between what is written and what the message is claimed to be.

3 The copying principle
Children imitate or copy letters or words to establish the first units of printed behaviour.

4 The recurring principle
Repeating an action helps in establishing quick, habitual response patterns and helps a child to realise that the same element can recur in variable patterns.

5 Directional principles
These relate to the understandings Giti (Baghban, 1984) had when she was 'writing' left to right and moving down the page. Clay claims that 'until some control has been gained over the directional principles the flexibility principle will be evident in the variety of approaches to print that children can devise' (p. 64).

6 Reversing the directional pattern
The child produces mirror writing.

7 The flexibility principle
Children experiment in creating new symbols by repositioning or decorating the standard forms.

8 The inventory principle
Children appear to take stock of their own learning by listing or ordering aspects of their literacy knowledge.

9 The generating principle
The child extends performance by knowing some elements and some rules for combining them to produce new statements in an inventive way.

10 The contrastive principle
Children create contrasts between shapes, meanings, sounds and word patterns.

11   The space concept
The child uses a space, or presumably some other symbol, to segment writing.

12   Page and book arrangement
The child, in addition to understanding the directional principle, can operate with larger areas of text.

13   The abbreviation principle
A child intentionally uses an abbreviation.

It is difficult to know quite what status is being given to these 'principles'. They clearly do not represent stages in any developmental sense. Clay is very specific about that: 'If there is an acquisition sequence which can be described for all children I have not been able to discover it in these examples' (Clay, 1975, p. 19). Regarding such differences in children's emerging writing she says: 'Such differences could be related to general intelligence but they could equally well occur because the experiences of the children have been different or because they have chosen to devote their attention to different aspects of their environment. I doubt whether there is a fixed sequence of learning through which all children must pass' (p. 7). Thus the 'principles' seem to be simply descriptions of some of the things emergent writers do. The principles do not govern becoming literate. All her samples were from children aged between four years ten months and seven years and her evaluations of them appear to be based on the documentation produced rather than on the circumstances in which the documentation occurred and the intentions of the writers. Thus it seems a fairly open question whether Clay's principles are consequences of the procedures used to examine the children's writing or whether they represent principles actually operated by children. They are certainly not the principles claimed by Harste, Burke and Woodward (1984) to be those on which children base their literacy behaviour, although there are clearly some relationships. Harste, Burke and Woodward identify 'risk taking', 'organisation', 'intentionality', and 'generativeness' as critical components of children's literacy, but are linked, by them, to social action, context, text and demonstrations.

The work of Clay (see also Quigg, 1985), and in particular Harste, Burke and Woodward, suggests very strongly that most children are, by the age of five, demonstrating through their writing that they have observed and understood a wide range of features of print production.

When a fluent user of written language composes a message, that user makes use of more elements than those discussed so far. The English language when written is represented through an alphabetic system. This system means that an infinite number of meanings can be represented by a relatively small number of elements. However, the limited number of elements used requires that the rendition of meaning is achieved partly through attention to the ordering of the elements. In English the 26 letters of our alphabet carry the major responsibility for conveying messages accurately. When reading it is possible to manage satisfactorily using many other cues to assign meaning to words (see Smith, 1971), but the writer has the burden of attempting to make explicit his message almost solely by the clear manipulation of the letters. The alphabetic nature of written English is not the easiest to learn, nor is it consistent in the way it represents spoken language. The history of literacy contains evidence of many attempts to simplify the task and make learning easier. The nature of the relationship between the way oral language operates and the way we write down language is not easy to perceive. It is the apparent difficulty of understanding this relationship which led to the inclusion of systematic and sequential instruction in the curriculum. Despite the problems it is now obvious that many children are, in their own ways, making successful attempts to bridge the gap between oral language and its representation in writing. Whereas Clay (1975) and Harste, Burke and Woodward (1984) deny the existence in their data of any developmental sequence in the way literacy emerges, there have been very strong claims for the existence of such sequences in the way children come to understand the alphabetic nature of written language (Henderson and Bears, 1980 and Ferreiro and Teberosky, 1983).

The seminal work in this area was a study by Read (1970) in which he investigated a group of pre-school children 'who invented their own spelling system for English, influenced relatively little by the standard system. In each case the child first learned the conventional names of letters of the alphabet; then with blocks or some other movable alphabet toy, began to spell words; and finally produced written messages of all kinds, including stories, letters and poems' (p. 3). This writing began as early as age three and a half and persisted into first grade. Read was able to write in 1971: 'Such spontaneous spelling is relatively rare' (p. 4). Today it would appear to be less rare than Read believed and allowing children to 'invent' their way to standard spelling is a fairly well-known technique (see Newman, 1984). Studies of invented spelling are now extensive, but the importance of Read's work was his discovery that children were placing great reliance on their phonological knowledge of English; they were attempting to break down spoken language, and secondly that orthographic knowledge appeared to be acquired systematically, not randomly. He believed that development in spelling, although strange to most adults' eyes, was, in fact, reasoned and sensible. Those children were actively constructing a writing system which, as their experience and knowledge increased, was modified many times resulting in a fair approximation to traditional orthography.

Henderson (1980) and his students and colleagues have spent many years looking at children's representation of written language. He claims: 'We have found further that children advance in their knowledge of words through discernible conceptual stages and that these stages hold with great stability across different methods of instruction, mixtures of dialect, and even different language' (p. 2). It is important to note that when Henderson writes about 'knowledge of words' he is mainly concerned with the way children 'compose' words and the way that as their understanding of what words are changes so 'their spelling errors change accordingly' (p. 10). Because of this preoccupation with words, Henderson gives little attention to many of Clay's principles and claims that at this early stage 'the most common production is one in which letters, invented letters, and numbers are set down in a jumble and in any direction' (p. 10). Such a conclusion would presumably surprise Clay and Harste. Henderson's claim is that as soon as a child has some kind of stable concept of a word, random, directionless inventions halt abruptly.

According to Henderson, children at first spell words 'by the phonemic feature that is emphasised in each letter as it is named in the alphabet of their language' (p. 11), or, presumably, within their culture; thus English children will spell 'leaf' as 'LEF', or as Bissex's (1980) son did, spell 'Genius at work' as 'GNYSATWRK'. Later comes what Henderson calls 'vowel transition'. This involves adding a silent letter or marker. Thus 'LEF' becomes 'LEIF' or 'LEFE'. The importance of this change is that it indicates a shift from a kind of one-to-one correspondence between the sound and its representation by a single letter, to an understanding that there are other underlying features in written language. It is Henderson's contention that invented spellings are intelligent creations by children, and that changes in those spellings occur systematically.

Such a view would certainly be shared by Ferreiro and Teberosky (1983) who start from the premise that children act on the world in intelligent ways. The children in their study were younger than those in the Henderson and Beers studies, but like those in the Harste, Burke and Woodward studies, came from a variety of social groups. Ferreiro and Teberosky claim to have identified five stages through which children pass as they emerge as writers. The first stage involves an intention to create a message and although the marks at all stages may look similar, a child would consider them to be different. At the first stage there appears to be a correspondence between quantifiable aspects of the object and the writing. Thus the 'name' for a big object will use more marks than a smaller object. There is often an interrelationship between drawing and writing although the two are used in different ways. 'Writing' is always linear and often cursive. If printing is used, a minimum of three characters is required before the child acknowledges it is writing rather than other kinds of marks. Ferreiro and Teberosky point out that the requirement of three letters as a minimum level of writing and the recognition of variation in the use of letters 'is strictly internal, that is, an outcome of children's ideas about writing' (p. 197). No adult will have taught them that words of two letters cannot be read.

At stage two the graphic form of the characters is more clearly defined and resembles conventional forms. Children at this level often use the few forms they know in a variety of combinations which seems to represent some discovery of the combinational quality of alphabetic language. Stage three is characterised by the child beginning to assign a sound value to each of the letters that compose a piece of writing. Ferreiro and

Teberosky call this the 'syllabic hypothesis' as they claim each letter stands for one syllable. The syllable-unit association is flexible and the same word may not receive the same syllable each time. The authors note that: 'The syllable hypothesis is an original construction of children and cannot be attributed to adult transmission' (p. 203).

Stage four marks the passage from the syllabic to the alphabetic hypothesis: 'The child abandons the syllabic hypothesis and discovers the need for an analysis that goes beyond the syllable' (p. 204). At this stage the child begins to use the properties of text (i.e. length, letters, segmentation) as cues. Children understand that there is a special relationship between the text and an oral reading of that text. Stage five, alphabetic writing, is the final achievement. 'They understand that each written character corresponds to a sound value smaller than a syllable and they systematically analyse the phonemes of the words they are writing' (p. 209). Children still have to learn the distinctive features of orthographic systems, i.e. spelling, as there are a large number of inconsistencies.

CONCLUSION

It seems clear that many children, given access to appropriate experience, demonstrate a commitment to writing, understand when and why much writing is used, and have some knowledge of how writing is carried out. As in the conclusion of Chapter 3, it must be acknowledged that although literacy is emerging in young children it may not emerge at the same rate in all children; thus by the time they arrive at school they will not all be at the same point. However, there seems no doubt that by the time many children reach the reception class they will have put some powerful intellectual effort into unravelling the phenomenon we call writing. Most children know

- that writing is a meaningful language activity;
- that its purpose is to communicate messages;
- that written language is composed of elements;
- that writing has certain forms and structures.

Many children, during those early years, are already exploring the use of written language to establish ownership and identity, to build relationships, to remember or recall, to request information, to record information, to fantasise or pretend, and to declare. All these aspects of written language use are recognised by Milz (1985) in her first-grade classroom. Children are not waiting for schooling in order to use writing in appropriate ways.

Children's knowledge may not be complete and the level of knowledge may not enable a child to engage in conventional communication, but nevertheless that knowledge does represent a significant level of emergent literacy: a level that has, for the most part, been achieved without conventional instruction. It has been achieved by observation, interaction and experimentation, and ought to provide a good base for learning to write conventionally. Unfortunately, conventional instruction with its specially 'simplified' sequences and systems often poses more problems than the complex world of written language has ever done.

5 Confusion or clarity

Downing (1979) states, as the fifth postulate of his 'cognitive clarity theory of reading', that: 'Children approach the task of reading instruction in a normal state of cognitive confusion about the purposes and technical features of language' (p. 36). Harste, Woodward and Burke (1984), however, assert quite emphatically that: 'After many years of work in this area ... we have yet to find a child who is cognitively confused' (p. 15). These contrasting views must be considered if the evidence of the previous two chapters is to be evaluated. Are the children who feature in those chapters cognitively confused or are they exhibiting cognitive clarity? How do Downing and Harste *et al.* arrive at such different conclusions? In order to evaluate these conflicting claims it is important to consider what lies at the heart of their viewpoints.

Downing's first specific declared interest in this area was prompted as a result of reading an article by Reid (1966). In this article Reid used a loosely structured interview to examine beginning readers' knowledge about reading. Twelve children were interviewed three times during their first year at school. Reid's interviews were an attempt to encourage children to talk rather than test in a formal sense. Reid opened with questions such as: 'Can you read yet?'; 'Have you any books at home?'; 'What is in them?'; 'Can your Mummy and Daddy read?'; 'How does Mummy know what bus to take?'; 'Can you write something for me?' According to Reid, the answers to those questions given by the children after two months in school showed a 'general lack of any specific expectancies of what reading was going to be like, of what the activity consisted in, of the purpose and use of it, of the relationship between reading and writing; and a great poverty of linguistic equipment to deal with new experiences' (*sic*) (p. 58).

By the second interview children were developing terminology and there was 'what might be called the beginning of a search for regularity and rule, and an awareness of the nature of an alphabetic system of writing' (p. 59). By the third interview children were moving 'to more refined or sophisticated notions' (p. 60) and 'awareness of phonic structure was developing' (p. 60). Reid makes a number of interesting points in her discussion. She says: 'Reading, prior to the experience is a mysterious activity, to which children come with only the vaguest of expectancies' (p. 60) and she clearly attributes any knowledge the children have to the instruction they had received: 'The earliest encounter with reading readiness training, phonic practice (initial letters and pictures) and writing had made them all aware, however, of a set of shapes' (p. 61). The origin of the 'confusion' label can be detected in her statement: 'These children can be seen therefore, as exhibiting certain linguistic and conceptual uncertainties about the nature of the material they had to organise' (p. 61), and she talks about children who 'groped' towards success.

Reid's paper was given great prominence by Downing who soon afterwards carried out a replication of Reid's work, but with some modifications. In a whole series of papers (Downing, 1969a; 1969b; 1970b; 1971; Downing and Oliver, 1974; Downing, Ollila and Oliver, 1975; Downing, Ollila and Oliver, 1977), he continued to explore children's understanding of reading and language, an area which has become well-known as part of 'metacognition' or 'metalinguistic awareness'. These complex sounding terms refer simply to that ability to use language, or thinking, to reflect upon language and thinking. In literacy these terms have often been associated with children's understanding of terms (for example, concepts such as 'word', 'letter', 'sound', and so on). Downing's work in this area culminated in the publication of the *Linguistic Awareness in Reading Readiness* test (Downing, Ayers and Schaffer, 1984).

In Downing's replication of Reid's study he introduced some concrete apparatus to replace the somewhat abstract nature of her questions. Specifically he had a model bus with a destination board and a model car with an 'L' plate on it. When the children in his study were asked to select the 'learner car', eight out of the thirteen children selected correctly. When they were asked, 'How do you know which bus to get on?' twelve out of the thirteen answered correctly. Despite this apparent success Downing felt able to declare that: 'Young beginners have serious difficulty in understanding the purpose of written language' (Downing, 1970a, p. 8). In general the results of this replication supported Reid's beliefs and Downing sums it up by saying that children 'have only vague expectations as to how people read, and they are especially confused by the use of abstract linguistic terminology' (1970a, p. 8). Downing links these difficulties with a view of reading as a skill. He uses a classification of Fitts and Posner (1967) and says that learning to read (and presumably learning to write) has three phases. The first is the 'cognitive phase' when the child has to work out what behaviour is relevant, and what are the techniques for dealing with the tasks involved. The second phase is the 'mastery phase' during which the skill is practised and mastery achieved. The third phase is the 'automaticity phase' during which the learner ceases to be a learner and can perform the skills unconsciously. He claims that the evidence 'strongly supports the existence of this cognitive phase in the initial stages of learning to read' (Downing, 1979, p. 35) but also admits that the 'cognitive phase, for example, is not limited to only the primary level of schooling' (1979, p. 35).

Downing's work in this area was not the only work to produce results which suggested that children's understanding of print was rather limited. Yaden (1984) reviewed over one hundred studies of young children's mctalinguistic awareness, all of which came to remarkably similar conclusions. He divided the papers into three areas. The first were studies of 'concepts about the nature, purposes and processes of reading' (and it should be noted that nearly all the studies he reviewed were concerned with reading rather than with reading and writing). All the studies in this section reported that beginning readers, and many who were beyond beginning, failed to see reading as a meaning gaining activity. He says: 'Indeed most studies indicated that the majority of students could not provide an intelligible description at all. Most other children viewed reading within the confines of a specific school-related task like learning the alphabet, doing work book pages, or retelling stories to the teacher' (Yaden, 1984, p. 14). The prize probably goes to the child who when asked what reading was said 'reading is stand-up, sit-down' (Johns, 1976/7).

Yaden's second section was 'concepts about spoken language units'. A great many of the studies were concerned with children's ability to segment their speech into units appropriate to written language. Such abilities underlie many of the sequential programmes for beginning reading. He says of those studies: 'Regardless of the method of data collection used, most studies indicated that a great number of primary aged children, as well as those with several years' schooling, were not able to analyse their speech into units such as phonemes or words, with some unable to distinguish between linguistic utterances and infrahuman sounds' (p. 26).

Yaden's final section was 'concepts about printed conventions'. He writes: 'There is remarkable unanimity in the findings that beginning readers do not possess firm concepts of printed language units such as letters, words or punctuation marks' (p. 34).

Yaden is forced to conclude from the evidence available to him (which was most of the formal metalinguistic studies) that: 'Beginning readers are largely unaware of the overriding structure of the writing system as well as their own speech. They have disparate notions as to what behaviour comprises the act of reading and the necessary steps that they must take in getting ready to become a reader' (p. 34). Yaden's conclusions after evaluating those studies would seem to correspond with Downing's views on young children's literacy competence.

There are, however, a number of issues that students of 'emergent' literacy would want to raise. The work on metalinguistic awareness derived initially from an interest in the way children became readers. It is in the nature of experimental investigation that the original function disappears in the apparent quest to examine smaller and smaller elements of metalinguistic behaviour. Almost imperceptibly it is children's performance in the experiments rather than their knowledge of reading that becomes the focus. Thus metalinguistic researchers became more interested in whether children could map bits of this to bits of that, than in whether children could actually perform as readers or writers. The research reviewed by Yaden shares a number of characteristics:

- Almost all the studies in this area are more concerned with awareness of terminology and abstract performance than whether children have any competence as readers and writers in an holistic sense.

- Almost all the investigations seem to assume that linguistic awareness is a necessary precondition of being able to read and write. However, as Yaden points out: 'Since ... the majority of studies have been correlational which have indicated a relationship between reading ability and metalinguistic awareness and have involved only statistical manipulations, it has been improper to tease out any definite temporal sequence' (p.36). In other words instead of metalinguistic awareness being necessary for development in literacy, it may be the case that it is development in literacy that causes an increase in metalinguistic awareness. Thus all the emphasis on metalinguistic awareness may be totally futile.

- Almost all the investigations produced their data from decontextualised testing situations frequently involving highly abstract questions or minute segments of activity that were supposed to be related to literacy. Few, if any, of those experiments seem to consider the way in which the nature of such situations poses framing problems for children, especially very young children. How are they supposed to behave when strangers come into the classrooms, remove them from the familiar environment and ask them to perform strange operations? Children desperately try to work out what it is that is required, but what is their view of such activities? What is their view of what they are doing? How are they supposed to interpret the requests of those strangers? The metalinguistic investigations on the whole, like many so-called literacy tests 'strip language of its context', and force children 'to deal with letters and words not only outside of a supportive linguistic environment, but also outside of a supportive context of situation' (Harste, Woodward and Burke, 1984, p. 9).

Even those studies which use apparently simple questions such as, 'What is reading?' (Tovey, 1976) pose immense problems not only for children but for adults as well. How would you, the reader of this book, react to the question 'What is reading?' Consider it as a problem for a five year old child, used to teachers asking questions which demand short answers and questions to which the child knows that the teacher has a specific answer.

- Following on from the previous point is the fact that hardly any of the many investigations cited by Yaden examined the child's behaviour in naturalistic settings where the child was allowed to demonstrate in his own way what he knew about literacy.

- Most of the investigations assume that because a child cannot give an adult-like response in a formal test situation he therefore does not know anything about literacy. However, it is worth remembering that the Hall *et al.* (1976) study did demonstrate that if you give children situations where they have the materials and the opportunity to use aspects of their literacy knowledge then they will demonstrate it.

- Almost without exception the results of these studies are reported in terms of what children cannot do. This is so even when there appears to be clear evidence that the children do have competence in some areas (see the Downing study cited earlier). Researchers persist in ignoring the positive scores made by children and concentrate on the failure of the children to perform with adult-like precision. Perhaps, as Goodman suggests, it is time to concentrate on how children have learnt what they do know. He says: 'We have been too preoccupied for too long with what children cannot do. We have lost the significance of what they have going for them that we can build on' (Goodman, 1976a, p. 23). Donaldson (1984) does warn that such an emphasis may be simply fashionable, but the problem for Donaldson would be finding schools that emphasise what children 'can do'. The evidence from classroom studies is that such schools are rare indeed.

- The final point is whether the cognitive confusion identified by Downing and supported by others exists in the child as a result of attempting to sort out literacy phenomena before it comes to school, or whether it is a consequence of being exposed to instructional categories and procedures which confound existing beliefs, not only about the content of the learning but also about the processes of learning. Many of the children who feature in metalinguistic experiments are already experiencing some schooling (particularly in the USA where kindergarten education is often formal) but rarely is this ever considered as a variable by researchers.

The seven points outlined above are not intended to show that Downing and the other metalinguistic researchers are wrong in identifying children as lacking complete understanding of the full literacy system and processes. They are intended to show how the subsequent negative view of children's literacy competence may be, to some extent, a consequence of the methods and attitudes of the researchers. If one looks for failure it is easy to find. The converse would also appear to be true. It seems that it may be a question of focus. As Goodman says : 'If anyone sees a half empty glass, adjust the focus so that it appears half-full' (Gollasch, 1982, p. 25). What happens when you adjust the focus? Is it still possible to see young children as cognitively confused? The response of Harste, Woodward and Burke, of the Goodmans, and of Ferreiro and Teberosky would appear to be an emphatic no. Indeed I suspect they would have a great deal of difficulty with the notion of 'confusion'. Confusion, for Downing, lasts a long time. It must, by definition, exist until the child has a conventional concept of all the literacy-related phenomena (although Downing does admit that 'confusion may recur' when one approaches certain higher level literacy skills); thus for several years between at least ages three to seven, children are cognitively confused because they are at what Downing calls the 'cognitive phase' in which the 'learner attends closely to the functions and techniques of the various tasks he must undertake to become a skilled performer' (Downing, 1979, p. 34). Is it the case that those children are suffering 'discomfiture, ruin, mental discomfort, embarrassment, perplexity, thrown into disorder, in tumult', all terms used by the *Shorter Oxford Dictionary* to describe confusion. Only one of nine definitions may fit Downing's use of confusion. It is 'failure to distinguish'. The difficulty with such a definition is that it renders us all confused, all of the time. Children know less about literacy than teachers, but teachers themselves know only a small part of what there is to be known about literacy. Does this mean that teachers are cognitively confused?

Of course, all teachers have seen children who are in 'discomfiture, ruin, mental discomfort', etc. where literacy is concerned. But is this the consequence of their learning process or of our teaching practices? There does seem a lot of evidence that the ways in which we behave and instruct are frequently themselves internally inconsistent, paradoxical and obscure.

The Goodmans, Ferreiro and Teberosky, and Harste *et al.* would, I am sure, claim that when children are left to sort out literacy in their own way they seldom experience 'discomfiture, ruin, mental discomfort' and so on. Of course, with literacy, as with all other aspects of the world, children will frequently experience events which challenge the beliefs they hold. This may create what Piaget called 'disequilibrium' or what Festinger termed 'cognitive dissonance'. But the consequence of those mental tensions is not a retreat into despair. It is difficult to imagine how intellectual development would occur if such experiences did not stimulate curiosity and a desire to create order.

The children in the investigations already cited in this book did not retreat into disorder when confronted with conflicting evidence about literacy. They evolved new ideas, new beliefs and new structures to account for the evidence. Perhaps this represents the fundamental difference between those who perceive children as confused and those who see them as competent. Downing's cognitive clarity model of reading is quite explicitly based on a view of learning to read as a skill. Ferreiro and Teberosky are also quite explicit. 'We refer to this learning as appropriation of knowledge, and not as the acquisition of a skill. As in any other domain of cognitive activity, appropriation is an active process of reconstruction carried out by knowing subjects' (1983, pp. 278–9). They also consider the consequences of such behaviour when it meets instruction. They say: 'To understand print, pre-school children have reasoned intelligently, elaborated good hypotheses about writing systems (although they may not be good in terms of our conventional writing system), overcome conflicts, searched for regularities, and continually attached meaning to written texts. But the logical coherence they impose on themselves disappears when faced with what the teacher demands from them. They must worry about perception and motor control instead of the need to understand. They must acquire a set of skills instead of coming to know an object. They must set aside their own linguistic knowledge and capacity for thought until they discover, at a later point, that it is impossible to comprehend a written text without them (1979, p. 279).

Similarly, Harste *et al.* (1984) reject the notion of literacy as simply a skill. Their analysis yields a picture of a language user handling many levels of information at any one time. Some of the methods employed may be novel, some well-known and understood, but always the event is handled in a way which anticipates it as a meaningful event. One aspect of language user behaviour which they identify as central is 'intentionality'. Intentionality is present whether the language user is producing or receiving text. It governs the way we receive text because our analysis of the context of use leads us to expect text which was intended for that particular setting. Intentionality equally governs what we produce because our productions are intended for particular situations. Harste, Woodward and Burke claim that: 'The importance of the assumption of intentionality is that it is a propelling force in literacy, setting in motion cognitive search strategies where significance can be deduced. Further, it is this very assumption which governs every literacy discovery from the initiate's very first insight to our own latest accomplishment' (1984, p. 191).

Thus for these authors there can be no three-level skill model progressing from confusion to clarity, or more precisely, from a cognitive phase to an automaticity phase. In Harste, Woodward and Burke's model of literacy, a child could be at all three levels at the same time; it is, therefore, from their point of view, not only unhelpful but quite wrong to conceive of children as cognitively confused. Because any language or literacy event operates on many levels, the participants' knowledge of, and mastery of, each level may be quite different, but because some levels are well understood 'their attention is freed to sort out still other patterns' (1984, p. 190).

For these authors there is no simple progressing from understanding form to understanding meaning, as implied in much of the metalinguistic research. As they say: 'Form clarifies and generates meaning, and meaning governs revision of surface text forms in both reading and writing' (1984, p. 200).

The last two paragraphs reveal the extent to which these authors feel that 'clarity' or 'proficiency' as an endpoint in learning more about literacy is non existent. At any point a learner can be both proficient and un-proficient, clear or unclear. As form influences meaning, and meaning in turn influences understanding of form, so the relationship will continu-ally shift. Thus, to go back to one of this chapter's opening quotations, Harste *et al.* can say that they have yet to find a child who is cognitively confused. What they do find, however, is children who are continuously inventing, discovering and changing their control over literacy events and processes.

The research of the Goodmans, and in particular Yetta Goodman, uncovers further evidence of children who are making sense of the world of literacy, rather than living in a state of perpetual confusion. The Goodmans do not suggest that children magically become literate, nor do they suggest that children inevitably become literate. As with Harste *et al.*, they recognise that progress towards literacy is a function of both experience and intelligent behaviour. The 'intelligent behaviour' which Y. Goodman (1983) calls 'self-teaching' occurs as part of an interaction with experience: 'This self-teaching happens only in literate societies and cultures where print bombards the senses of children' (p. 69). She suggests that intelligent behaviour towards literacy phenomena is guided by searching for meaning. 'The important questions for children seem to be, "What is written language for?", "What does it mean?" Through this kind of exploration, children begin to make all kinds of intuitive decisions about how written language means' (p. 70).

The consequence of an interreaction between experience and intelli-gent behaviour is the construction of 'rules' or 'principles' to account for the things experienced, and as experience continues (and of course future experience includes reflection on the 'principles' already formed, and their application), the principles are modified or even discarded. As K. Goodman (1985) points out: 'As with the development of all principles, it is clear that some of the principles children develop will be partially developed, non-productive, or far from the actual principles of written language. But these represent their own active search for order in their world and it is through their mistakes that they learn' (p. 60). Clearly there will often be a rather individual flavour to those principles as the experiences of children can be different: 'These principles, I believe, emerge idiosyncratically for each child. Some principles may be con-sidered together from the beginning and others may not. Children may reject one principle for another, depending on the text, the item, the significance of the reading or writing experience to the child, or the function of any particular literacy event' (Y. Goodman, 1983, p. 74).

The existence of such 'child-constructed principles' takes us back to the relationship between the emergence of oral language and the emergence of literacy as outlined in Chapter 2. Several of the elements of that relationship were clear in Chapter 2: parents facilitate the emergence of both oral language and literacy but seldom do it through direct instruction; children experience oral language and literacy through other activities; children experience both oral and written language in ways which are similar to their experience of other aspects of the world; becoming orate and becoming literate both depend on social interaction; and the child's experience of both oral and written language is essentially holistic. It should now be clear that there are powerful relationships between the remaining principles of oral language learning outlined in Chapter 2 and the emergence of literacy. It seems that, prior to formal schooling, children play the major role in constructing their knowledge of both written and oral language. In Chapters 3 and 4 evidence was presented of young children interacting with print and formulating ideas about how written language worked. The children may often have been wrong and they may have needed to understand much more, but the effort had been put into constructing hypotheses to account for the phenomenon that we call literacy.

It seems equally clear that the emergence of literacy and the emergence of oral language constitute attempts to comprehend and create meanings. It is in the pursuit of meaning that both oral and written language emerge. Children expect print to make sense and they expect their own writings to make sense. The utterance 'What does that say?' is used not only with reference to print in the environment or print in books, but, early on, is frequently used in respect of children's own marks.

Finally, the experience children have of both written and oral language allows them to regulate aspects of their lives and in turn to understand the regulation of their lives by others. When children experience events like shopping lists and the subsequent shopping they can begin to understand both the power to create print and the power print can have once it has been created.

The evidence from the work of Ferreiro and Teberosky, Harste et al., and the Goodmans would seem to suggest that children can no longer be seen as inevitably deficient or in a state of cognitive confusion. It would seem to be confusion itself to confound 'failure to have conventional knowledge' with 'confusion'. However, it depends on how you happen to focus on the glass. Do you see it as half-empty or half-full? Everyone agrees that children have a far from complete knowledge of literacy by the time they arrive in school, whether in the United Kingdom, the United States, Argentina or Australia. The difference in accounts is the status given to the 'incomplete' performance of children. Should it be seen as evidence of success, or should it be seen as evidence of failure? One might ask, 'Does it make any difference how you see it?' I would suggest it could certainly make a difference whether you approached children by considering them competent, or whether you approached them as incompetent. If the result of children's own learning about literacy is 'incompetence' then perhaps children need exposure to alternative strategies for becoming literate. If, however, the result of children's own learning is 'competence' then perhaps one should look for teaching strategies which perpetuate the circumstances that have allowed competence to develop.

6 Monitoring emerging literacy

There is no shortage of tests for use in assessing reading. However, few are designed for assessing writing. Amongst those tests for assessing reading are many intended to examine 'reading readiness', but almost all those tests and profiles share the assumptions underlying instruction outlined at the beginning of Chapter 1. To examine most reading readiness tests is to discover a catalogue of perceptual items, both visual and auditory. It is extremely uncommon to find reading readiness tests that reduce to anything relating to normal literacy behaviour. For that reason, and because it has been a consistent belief expressed in this book that atomistic skills are not a necessary condition for learning to read and write, such tests will not be considered. Instead this chapter considers, first, two relatively formal tests which were designed to relate more precisely to literacy behaviour, and, secondly, whether procedures other than formal testing might be more useful in monitoring the emergence of literacy.

The tests and procedures discussed in this chapter are considered in the context of nursery and infant classrooms, as those are the most likely places of use experienced by readers of this book. They could, of course, be used in other situations where adults want to enquire about children's emergent literacy, for example, at home or in clinics.

MARIE CLAY'S *CONCEPTS ABOUT PRINT* TEST

The *Concepts About Print* test is a relatively simple examination of some aspects of reading and print knowledge which are not covered by conventional reading readiness tests. It is important to note though that Clay denies emphatically that this test is a 'readiness' test. She says: 'It reveals some of the behaviours that are related to reading progress but only a very few of them' (Clay, 1982, p. 87). The test is available in two versions, *Sand* (Clay, 1972) and *Stones* (Clay, 1979a). The instructions for administration and interpretation are contained in another book by Clay (1979c). The test is strictly related to reading and was designed for children starting the formal process of reading instruction. She comments: 'The test reflects changes in reading skill during the first year of instruction but is less significant in the subsequent years for children who make average progress' (Clay, 1979c, p. 17). Despite this claim the test can be used with much younger children (I have used it with three year olds) although as indicated by Hartley and Quine (1982) in their review of the test, it is only parts of the test which normally have application at that age.

The test consists of a twenty-page booklet which looks like a simple story book. It has text on one page and an illustration on the facing page for each spread except the centre spread. The appearance of the booklet is deceptive because as the story progresses odd things begin to happen: illustrations invert; text inverts; lines, words and letters are mixed up, and so on. This has clearly confused some purchasers of the test as the publishers have found it necessary to insert a slip informing people that these unconventional aspects are intentional. To use the test the administrator sits down with an individual child and claims that he/she is going to read the story but wants the help of the child. The child is then asked a series of questions about the book. The instructions identify twenty areas of knowledge to be examined. Goodman (1981, p. 446) has conveniently and concisely grouped these areas as follows:

1 *Concepts about book orientation*
Items related to these concepts provide insights into whether children know how to open books, and know when a book, pictures or print are correctly oriented.

2 *Concepts about whether print or pictures carry the text message*
These are observed by asking children to point to where the observer is reading as the observer reads aloud.

3 *Concepts about directionality of lines of print, page sequences, and directionality of words*
These are evaluated by asking children to follow with a finger and point as the teacher reads and also by asking them to say what is wrong with a page that has lines of print, letters or words out of order.

4 *Concepts about the relationship between written and oral language*
The children are asked to follow with a finger as the observer reads. This provides insight into their awareness of what is being read and how that relates to the words being spoken.

5 *Concepts of words, letters, capitals, space and punctuation*
These are obtained by asking the children what the conventions are, or asking them to point to such items

The test has been standardised on very small samples in New Zealand and Texas (although the full details of the reference cited are missing from the 1979c book by Clay) and in Clay (1979c) there is a table showing European children's age expectations for test items. Unfortunately, no details are given on what evidence this table was constructed. However, Clay does point out that it is not as a standardised test that the test has most value: 'The test's greatest value is diagnostic. Items should uncover concepts to be learned or confusions to be untangled' (Clay, 1979c, p. 18).

When the test appeared it represented an interesting departure from conventional reading readiness tests. However, it is not without its problems. Hartley and Quine (1982) examined its use with 42 children and found a number of disturbing factors. They decided that the instructions were confusing to many children and that the instructions confounded the expectations of the children. Hartley and Quine claim that: 'Expecting to hear a story, the child finds the narrative is interrupted page after page by what must seem quite irrelevant questions ... it is not surprising that a number of testees observed that it was a "funny" or "silly" book' (p. 110). They point out that some children failed to point correctly to the bottom of the inverted picture yet in discussion afterwards those same children said they knew it was upside down. These children had clearly found the instructions ambiguous. Thus it was the language of the test which was problematic – not the concept of inversion. Hartley and Quine list a number of problems of this kind and they develop a number of interesting questions about the test. Most of those questions relate to the testing procedure and test construction.

Goodman (1981) also reviewed this test and while acknowledging its novel approach was, like Hartley and Quine, less than happy about the standardised form of its administration. Somewhat confusingly Goodman praised it for being: 'The first instrument I have seen which uses a real reading experience' (p. 447), but later criticised the booklet for being 'unnatural'. She said 'The upside down print and pictures, and the words, sentences and letters out of order ... are not natural to the text and even good readers may miss those because they don't expect such aberrations', which was exactly the implication of many of Hartley and Quine's comments.

Goodman does, however, suggest a way around some of these problems. She suggests that 'researchers and teachers should explore using the test booklets in different ways' (p. 447). She also suggests that once teachers familiarise themselves with the ideas implicit in the test they could adapt most of those ideas for use with any picture/story book. Thus Goodman is essentially suggesting that teachers use the ideas as a basis for observing literacy behaviour, rather than remaining tied to the standardised administration procedures. When Goodman's observations are put alongside those of Hartley and Quine it does seem that the problems inherent in the standardised procedures limit the knowledge that can be gained. However, it does have some advantages in its speed, and ease of administration. For people working with young children the test provides a relatively simple and quick way of allowing some aspects of literacy behaviour to be observed.

THE *LINGUISTIC AWARENESS IN READING READINESS* TEST

John Downing's interest in linguistic awareness and his views about the importance of cognitive confusion as a factor in literacy failure have led him and co-workers to devise a test which examines this aspect of literacy development. The origins of this test can, as was indicated in the previous chapter, be traced back to Downing's work in England at the end of the 1960s, but in a more precise form the development of the test is indicated in Evanechko, Ollila, Downing and Braun (1973), Downing, Ollila and Oliver (1975), Downing, Ayers and Schaffer (1978), and Ayers and Downing (1982). These studies resulted in the publication of the *Linguistic Awareness in Reading Readiness* test (Downing, Ayers and Schaffer, 1983), known as LARR. The LARR test attempts to measure: 'Children's linguistic awareness and their concepts of reading and writing, and the functions and features of these skills' (Downing, Ayers and Schaffer, 1983, p. 1). The test consists of three booklets.

1 Recognising literacy behaviour

In this section a child is assessed on his/her ability to recognise the kinds of acts that constitute literacy activities. For instance, in one section of this booklet the child is asked to draw a ring around each person (out of four illustrations) who is reading. In another section a child is asked to circle things that can be read. The idea is to see if a child can distinguish between reading text and, for example, looking at pictures, or if it can distinguish between materials that need reading rather than just looking at. Downing *et al.* believe that success on this sub-test is vital. They believe that 'the child can hardly learn to read and write if he or she does not know what "reading" and "writing" are' (p. 2).

2 Understanding literacy functions

In this section the child is asked to identify the purposes for which people read and write. For instance, in one part, faced with a set of illustrations of people performing literacy acts, the child is asked to circle each person who is finding out what shows are on TV. Downing, Ayers and Schaffer (1983) believe that understanding these functions is the: 'Foundation of flexible reading that enables the reader to vary his or her strategies according to the purpose of the reading act and the difficulty of the text' (p. 2). It is interesting to note that literacy has suddenly become reading, even though many of the examples feature writing events.

3 The technical language of literacy

In this section the child is assessed on his/her knowledge of the technical terms used to describe written language. A whole range of technical language is covered: number; letter; capitals; top-line; first word; question marks, and so on – thirty examples in all.

The LARR test is, unlike Clay's *Concepts About Print* test, a readiness test. 'To benefit from instruction in reading and writing the pupil must understand the functions of those literacy skills and must comprehend such concepts as "word", "letter", "top-line", and so on' (Downing, Ayers and Schaffer, 1983, p.1). The significant word in this quotation is instruction. If the child achieves a certain level of competence then he/she is ready to profit from formal instruction. It will be clear from earlier chapters that this represents a controversial view of literacy development. Despite the 'readiness' tag the LARR test has a more general function of informing the assessor about the child's competence in some elements of literacy. Whether one adopts a Downing 'readiness' perspective, or whether one has a more generally developmental notion of literacy, the test has, in principle, the potential to inform.

There are, however, some important points about LARR that must be considered in evaluating its usefulness. Unlike the *Concepts About Print* test, LARR is a very formal looking test and it takes a long time to administer. It can (it is claimed) be used to assess whole groups of children at once, and it is designed for use with children at a certain level of competence.

The formality of a test like LARR is quite outside the experience of most four and five year olds in Britain. I have used the test with four year olds but some of them were clearly puzzled about what to do, and resolved their bewilderment by adopting strategies that from the test's perspective resulted in nil scores. When these children were afterwards taken back to the test and individual items were discussed it was evident that they knew a great deal more about literacy than the results suggested. A particular example will make this clear. One child when tested on the 'technical language of literacy' section scored almost nothing. Afterwards, as the child's name was being written on the cover of the test booklet the child said: 'My name's not spelled like that – it's spelled M A T T E W'. What is one to make of the discrepancy between this behaviour and the apparent results of the test? The issue is really a very similar one to that raised by Goodman (1981) and Hartley and Quine (1982) in respect of the *Concepts About Print* test; is the form of the testing and the structure of the test actually interfering with the expression of the knowledge which the tests were designed to reveal?

The test takes about an hour to administer. Ideally each section should be administered on different days. Even so, twenty or twenty-five minutes seems a long to time to ask a four or five year old to concentrate on a single, narrow activity. However, I must report that I have not yet come across a child who has lost interest in the activity. It would appear that children do not find it boring. Certainly there is plenty to look at. The authors claim that the test can be administered to large groups but do recommend that in that case a second adult should be present.

The test is essentially designed to be used with children between the ages of four and six. Thus items which did not appear to function usefully for this age group were discarded as the test was developed. Within this age group it has been well tested in Canada and there is some data on predictive validity. It would seem that part three is the most powerful predictor of future reading ability ('future' meaning one year after the administration of LARR). However, in a few cases part one was the best predictor. This difference raises a rather significant point. Is the predictive validity related not to the 'learning of literacy' but to the method of instruction? If a child is in a class which stresses a phonic approach (as most North American schools do), then perhaps the relationship between part three and reading success is not surprising. It would be interesting to know if the classrooms where part one was the best predictor of success used a more holistic approach. Clearly some investigation is needed here. It is also important to note that the relationships explored were with reading. LARR also uses many items related to writing but possible relationships in this area have not been explored. The critical issue is whether LARR assesses knowledge about literacy, or whether it assesses knowledge about literacy instruction. With younger children this may not be a problem but with children already at school the results would need to be interpreted with caution.

The LARR test is undoubtedly novel in the way it explores a number of areas absent from other 'readiness' tests: it raises, for teachers, new issues to think about. However, almost all the teachers I know who have tried it, or considered it seriously, are convinced they would be unlikely to use it. One teacher described it as 'using a sledgehammer to crack a nut'. There was a general feeling amongst those teachers that a reasonable teacher using observational techniques would find out more about a child's literacy than would be gained by using LARR, and would do so in circumstances that were more genuine in terms of the child's use of literacy. In this respect teachers found LARR useful in alerting them to look at certain areas of behaviour. More than a few teachers suggested that the list of areas noted on the score sheets formed a useful checklist.

A group of teachers I have worked with have used the test booklets in another way. Just as Yetta Goodman (1981) suggested that teachers use the *Concepts About Print* test as an observational tool, so some teachers have found it more useful to use the test, not in its formal role, but as a basis for general discussion with the children. Thus instead of asking for a simple response the teacher is able to follow up, and probe, children's responses. Used in this way one forgets about normative data and treats the test as an interesting print item, just as one might use any other print item as a discussion point with children. The age of the child becomes largely irrelevant when used in this way: it could be used with all ages and abilities in circumstances where it was felt, by the teacher, that some illustrations of print-related behaviour would be helpful.

'KIDWATCHING'

It has already been implied in the discussion of CAP and LARR that their usefulness may be greatly extended if the formal element is forgotten and the elements of the tests used simply as a basis for discussion and observation.

In one sense formal testing is 'observation' of children. Children are given something to do and their response is observed and recorded. There are, however, some limitations with formal tests, limitations which, while not negating their usefulness in certain specific situations, often mean that the knowledge gained about children is limited.

Most tests, including many non-standardised tests, have specific procedures for administration. The questions which are asked and the way in which they are asked, is carefully controlled. That is certainly the case in CAP and LARR. However, as we have already seen, some children fail to display what they know because of something in the test, its administration, or its context of use. Assuming one uses a test because one wants to know more about the way a particular child thinks and behaves, then the experience must allow them to demonstrate their abilities, not inhibit them from showing competence.

Another problem with formal tests is that they are, quite properly, designed to elicit specific information about a child. This is a strength of a test, but for a classroom teacher such specificity is often limiting unless the teacher is totally clear about the information required. Teachers often need and want much more than the specific information elicited by a test. However, as tests are, for the most part, relatively easy to administrate, and as they have been designed by 'experts', it can be tempting to use them without question regardless of whether they really give you the knowledge you require.

A third problem with formal testing is that tests are usually experienced by children outside the context in which the behaviours being tested normally occur. Thus testing is, for a child, a somewhat strange experience. Many studies of children's behaviour have shown how important the context is for regulating children's performance.

The three 'problem' areas are not a criticism of tests as such, simply a reminder that tests have highly specific uses and are only suited to those situations where those uses match the requirements of the teacher. For teachers in classrooms there will often be a mismatch between information required and tests, as the planning and implementation of curriculum decisions demands the widest and most thorough understanding possible of the nature, knowledge and experience of every individual child in a classroom. The stress on 'individual' is important as frequently one of the unfortunate consequences of formal testing is the reduction of an individual to a statistic. As Wolf and Tymitz (1976) point out: 'In our search for generalisable knowledge, we tend to treat everyone or every situation as the same. We fail incessantly to honor uniqueness in our fervour to understand commonness. But anyone who has spent time in real educational settings understands how these artifacts of measurement distort seriously the realities of classroom life'. Perhaps Kenneth Goodman summed it up when he stated in respect of investigations into reading: 'Of what value is it to prove everyone does something if understanding how one person does it is what we really need to know' (Goodman, 1976a).

It is the recognition of the limitations of formal testing (and more formal research procedures) that have led many people to suggest, and develop, strategies which rely more on broad observation of children's behaviour and analysis of those observations. Such procedures are particularly helpful where emerging literacy is concerned as there are so few relevant formal test instruments. Clay reacts against some of the problems of formal testing when she says: 'Teachers are unlikely to make such gross averaging judgements about children's needs when they work alongside individual children, observing their responses and using techniques which increase the sensitivity of their observation. Under these circumstances teachers will arrive at more insightful assumptions and make fewer naive or superficial ones' (Clay, 1982).

Such insightful and reflective observation has been termed 'Kidwatching' by Yetta Goodman, and such strategies underlie the success of Action-Research in British schools. In 'Kidwatching' Goodman stresses not only observations of children but also interaction with children, and observation of the environment. 'Kidwatching' is, of course, ideally suited to learning about very young children. Y. Goodman (1985) identifies three basic premises upon which notions of 'Kidwatching' are built:

1   Observers must have a framework for making sense of what they see. Seeing is not a neutral activity: it is a response to our beliefs, attitudes, values and knowledge. With different types of knowledge observations can be perceived in different ways. The establishment of a framework based on sound understanding cannot be underestimated. As Goodman says: 'Current knowledge about child language and conceptual development must be part of continuous education for teachers. Such knowledge guides observations. Not only does it help teachers know what to look for but it also helps teachers become consciously aware of their knowledge, their biases, and their philosophical orientation' (Goodman, 1985, p. 11).

2   Observers must watch children in a wide range of contexts. What one can observe depends on the freedom of children to engage in a wide variety of activities. Children who are sitting at desks filling in blank spaces will not demonstrate the range of behaviours, as noted by Hall et al. (1986) when they filled a 'home corner' with a multitude of print-related items and sat back and watched. Prior to this intervention it would have been easy to identify these children as uninterested in written language. As Goodman points out: 'Language and concepts grow and develop depending on the settings in which they occur, the experiences that children have in those settings, and the interaction of the people in those settings. The richer and more varied these settings and interactions, the richer the child's language and concepts will be' (Goodman, 1985, p. 11).

3   Observers must also examine their own role in the literacy events. Language learning whether oral or written is an interactive process. In classrooms and homes, adults are part of this process and it is their behaviour which is a major contributor to the ways in which children think about literacy. For that reason observers have to reflect on their own behaviour, not just that of the child. As adults continuously intervene in children's behaviour so the adults' behaviour must be continuously monitored, as well as its interaction with that of the children.

To Goodman's three premises I would add a fourth and a fifth:

4   It is important not to accept observations at face value. Because 'seeing' is a product of theory it can be all too easy to simply 'see' what we already believe. Observation is of no value whatsoever unless it has the potential to lead to a change in belief. It doesn't have to – the observation may confirm belief; however teachers must always be ready to go beyond the initial assumptions about what they see. It comes as a surprise to many student teachers that children think differently from adults and although teachers know that in a formal sense, they frequently fail to see that children might think differently from them about a particular activity. Therefore, a critical question for observers of children's behaviour is to ask, 'What was it that the child believed which led it to behave like that?' In other words, to go back to one of Harste, Woodward and Burke's central concerns, 'What was the child's intention?' Considering intention in literacy demands thought not only about linguistic rules for producing or receiving written language, but also about the social understanding of children. The behaviour of children is governed not only by their knowledge of structure, but also by the settings where structures can be used.

5   Have patience! Observation requires time. An observer must be prepared to wait for long periods of time and not be easily defeated. With 'Kidwatching' one is observing behaviour in as many different contexts as possible and over as much time as possible. Therefore one must be prepared to wait rather than jump to the conclusion that children do not know something or are unable to act in certain ways.

To these premises must be added the corollary 'do not believe in certainty'. We cannot get inside children's minds: we can only extrapolate from observed behaviours. Thus all our conclusions are, at best, tentative. The imperative in 'Kidwatching' must be to stay alert for all clues, observe consistently and always be prepared to modify conclusions.

By looking closely at classrooms or homes, by becoming acute observers, and by using 'Kidwatching' techniques (TAWL, 1984), teachers, parents and researchers may well learn not simply about the way literacy is emerging in their children but also about the ways in which they, as adults, are interacting with the children and the environment to facilitate the emergence of literacy.

7 Emergent literacy and schooling

INTRODUCTION

The previous chapters have recorded some of the evidence which demonstrates that children are neither 'empty vessels' waiting to be filled with literacy once they have arrived at school, nor 'passive recipients' being stuffed with literacy by parents and teachers. In summary children create their literacy in contexts where: literacy is a meaningful event for them; where they see people participating in literacy for real purposes and with enjoyment; where people are prepared to discuss their literacy activities; where there are opportunities for children to participate in literacy; where child-initiated literacy behaviour is welcomed by adults; and where children's literate efforts are treated seriously.

Are these features of the situations created within schools for teaching children to become literate? Does literacy continue to emerge or is it likely that children will meet a highly artificial approach to literacy instruction which will force them to abandon their previous knowledge and beliefs?

TRANSITION INTO SCHOOLING

The learning achieved by young children demands respect. In the almost total absence of explicit instruction, children move from a state of almost complete helplessness to a stage where they are articulate reasoning human beings, constructing many complex hypotheses about the way the world works. The rate of learning during the first four or five years of life is probably unequalled in the remainder of people's lifetimes. As Bissex points out: 'Children are small; their minds are not' (Bissex, 1984, p. 100).

The move from the world of home is a complex one and for many children it may represent the first major upheaval in their life. This is true whether the move be to nursery school or directly into a reception class. The changes experienced by the child are dramatic and this would seem to apply as much to their experiences of literacy as to any other aspects of their lives. From the evidence available, it would appear that the contrast between the kind of environment where literacy has been emerging, and the school environment is considerable.

What actually happens when children go to school? Are they able to continue to construct their ideas about literacy in a meaningful manner? Are they going to have a wide range of purposeful literacy behaviours demonstrated to them? Are they going to experience the same kind of facilitative discussion? Are they going to experience an environment where they can participate in a variety of purposeful literacy activities? Will they continue to see literacy used as a means of enriching lives? Are children going to experience an environment which supports their interpretation of text and their production of writing? Are they going to be allowed to sort out their own rules for interpreting and organising print for their own social purposes? Will the school environment enable children to continue to understand that: 'Literacy events function not as isolated bits of human activity but as connected units embedded in a functional system' (Anderson and Stokes, 1984)? Are they going to be exposed to the fifty types of print encountered in homes by Leichter (1984), participate in events as dynamic as the example of the bulletin board cited in Chapter 2, or engage in such personally relevant literacy activities as the example of Pauline and her mother working on their shopping list (Tizard and Hughes, 1984)?

In many schools, all over the world, the answer to those questions would appear to be no! A range of evidence seems to point to schools providing an environment which conflicts with many young children's beliefs about, and expectations for, print and its use. It appears that schools, far from continuing to open options about literacy, frequently operate effectively to close such options down. Even the nursery school, which as an institution has a reputation for focusing on the child and providing an environment for rich, explorative and imaginative play, modifies children's behaviour in a limiting way. Tizard and Hughes (1984) when writing of the 'talk' in the nursery school that they observed state:

> When we came to analyse the conversations between these same children and their nursery teachers, we could not avoid being disappointed. The children were certainly happy at school, for much of their time absorbed in play. However, their conversations with their teachers made a sharp contrast to those with their mothers. The richness, depth and variety which characterised the home conversations was sadly missing. So too was the sense of intellectual struggle, and of the real attempts to communicate being made on both sides. The questioning, puzzling child which we were so taken with at home was gone: in her place was a child who, when talking to staff, seemed subdued, and whose conversations with adults were mainly restricted to answering questions rather than asking them, or taking part in minimum exchanges about the whereabouts of other children and play materials (p. 9).

From those children's school lives was missing much of the intellectual effort which at home they put into sorting out the world, and also the quality of oral interaction so important in facilitating development. Those two aspects represent a significant part of the conditions necessary for the continued emergence of literacy. Tizard and Hughes also showed that in the school they observed teachers felt parents should model themselves on teachers; that teachers inhibited much decision-making and negotiating behaviour; that teachers asked questions rather than engaged in conversations; that talk was mainly about play rather than the rich variety of situations that were discussed at home; and that teachers were more intent on pursuing their own educational aims than offering children the chance to explore the world at their own level. Such an analysis makes the school sound a poor one which was clearly far from the case. As will be discussed later in this chapter, schools do have different functions from homes and it is inevitable, and reasonable, that children will experience many differences.

Such problems are not just the concern of British nursery schools. Juliebo (1985) studied a group of children's literacy behaviours at home and at a Canadian kindergarten school. She identified five major differences between home and school:

- In the home the child was the main initiator of literacy learning whereas in school the teacher was the initiator and the children's attempts to initiate were not accessed.

- At home, sharing and reciprocity were constantly manifest. In the kindergarten, in general, the children had to reciprocate in the predetermined programme, the construction of which was not mutually shared between teacher and learner.

- Many activities in the kindergarten were only concerned with the here and now and precluded transcendence. This was particularly true of work time and art activities. At home transcendence was present in most children's literacy interactions.

- At school literacy activities were not grounded in the children's own lifeworlds and as a result often lacked meaning. This was in strong contrast to the home where literacy was a part of everyday life. Interactions in the home were almost always accompanied by a joyful sharing.

- In the home environment constant feedback was given to encourage feelings of competence. In the school errors were often corrected without explanations. (Juliebo, 1985, pp. 132–3)

From Juliebo's study it was also clear that many of the conditions under which literacy was emerging at home, disappeared at school, even at 'preschool' level. The difficulties may be compounded for children who go directly to infant schools. It would appear that literacy, in infant classrooms, can too often appear as anything but personally meaningful and relevant out of school.

Hodgson and Pryke (1983) set out to observe and talk to teachers of children aged six and ten. The report was rather misleadingly titled *Reading competence at 6 and 10*; it was actually concerned with finding out 'about the link between teacher perception and teacher practices in the teaching of reading' (p. 1).

The major finding of the report was that the teachers were almost totally obsessed with systematic and sequential approaches to the teaching of reading; approaches based on a deficit model and the remediation of this deficit by programmes of systematic instruction. The authors say: 'There is very little evidence of any sort of contextual approach to the teaching of reading' (p. 15), and: 'There was no indication that any of the teachers interviewed perceived reading as a process' (p. 34). The results of such teaching created problems: 'Indeed the methods they adopt, because they are essentially mechanistic, often militate against the child actually enjoying reading' (p. 35). All the quotations used in this review of their paper relate to the teachers of the six year olds.

The most dominant feature of the teaching was the 'listening to children read' sessions. During these sessions the 'most favoured method shown by this sample of infant teachers was direct intervention when a child made a decoding error' (p. 19). Interruptions were frequent and: 'The whole activity seems to be conducted in a perfunctory manner where the main objective is to hear the next child read' (p. 15).

The activities of the teachers in this sample almost seem to represent a conspiracy to create a model of reading that is just about as far as one can get from any notions of reading being a useful social activity, relevant to all aspects of life. As in nursery schools, the children's language was neglected: 'The overwhelming majority of the teachers in the sample did not appear to use a child's spoken or written language as a resource for reading' (p. 38). The teachers appeared to segment the world in such a way that the reading of books was made to appear less important than many other activities: 'When they have done their work they can get books anytime' (p. 48). Hodgson and Pryke are forced to conclude: 'We came to wonder whether the competence of the reader was being influenced more from outside school than within it. What concerns us about the content of some of the reading materials in use in schools is that they may give impressions of reading which turn children away from reading for pleasure rather than draw them to it' (p. 6), and they were concerned that the approach of teachers in their survey which was what they termed a 'deficit' model resulted in children 'who spent much time doing things which they did not need and which were of little value anyway' (p. 4).

Those comments, and others in the report, indicate the failure on the part of those teachers to provide mental space, social interaction, meaningful contexts for reading, discussion about reading, and perhaps most worrying of all, encouragement. It is easy to see how such contexts baffle and deflect many children whose previously emerging views about reading made sense. The situation regarding writing may be little different. Bennett, Desforges, Cockburn and Wilkinson (1984) investigated the extent to which teachers of top infant children managed to match the tasks they set to the needs of the pupils. The sample of teachers was selected by the Local Education Authority who claimed that they represented above average teachers. One chapter in their study is devoted to the language curriculum. The researchers discovered that:

There was no evidence of an integrated curriculum in operation in any of the classrooms studied (p. 99).

The predominant aim expressed in more than 70% of tasks intended to promote writing was to 'practise' writing, and to use some aspect of grammar, especially capital letters and full stops as sentence markers (p. 101).

It was impossible to distinguish between tasks aimed at developing imaginative writing and tasks aimed at writing reports (p. 103).

Finding the correct answers was exceedingly straightforward and the vast majority of time on these tasks was spent recording responses, a procedure which was little more than further writing practice (p. 119).

Requests for spellings constitute the predominant teacher/pupil exchanges in language lessons (p. 128).

As the authors point out: 'The findings reveal that despite the conscientious efforts of able teachers a number of serious issues are apparent, some of which appear to be hidden from the teachers.' Further evidence comes from the HMI study of first schools in England (DES, 1982). Two summary comments illustrate the problems for children: 'In almost all schools the youngest children were introduced too quickly to published reading schemes and phonic practice with the result that some were confused and made little progress' (p. 5), and: 'Copying from workbooks and cards occupied too great a part of the time of some 5 and 6 year olds' (p. 12).

The consequence of such experiences is that children are exposed to quite a different set of assumptions from those operating prior to entry to school. As Bennett et al. (1984) point out: 'Intended classroom learning is embedded in the tasks teachers provide for children'. When those tasks are narrowly defined then there is a considerable difference from the pre-school experience of literacy at home where literacy events 'were embedded within the routine and social interactions of adults and children' (Schieffelin and Cochran-Smith, 1984, p. 7).

One specific consequence of such classroom experiences is that children's notions of what literacy is change. Dyson (1985) quotes Callie, a kindergartener who replied when asked why adults write: 'Big people,' she said, 'Got to write to show the people – the little people – what to write.' More specifically, 'They write alphabet that we folks write, little folks' (p. 498). The tautologous reasoning that children learn to write so that as 'big folks' they can teach 'little folks' to write is not uncommon. Another kind of reasoning was identified by one of my students. She (an experienced class teacher) had a discussion with her children about why people read and write. In an effort to help her class she told them that she kept a book by the side of her bed and asked why. After a pause for thought one child answered: 'So you can practise.' When she told them that she didn't have to practise there was general disbelief until one child produced a book with what appeared to the child to contain very difficult writing. 'Go on, read that then,' he said. She told me that for several days children kept bringing in apparently difficult print items for her to read in order to test her statement that she did not have to practise reading. Had those children thought that there was a lifetime ahead of 'practising reading' or did they think that she, as a teacher, had to practise reading?

Such experiences are not confined to Britain. Bissex wrote of her son that it was no wonder that Paul, a child who was at home performing complex phonic exchanges 'had a difficult time completing workbook exercises the next year when he was in first grade. The playfulness and sense of discovery was gone and he was not interested in demonstrating what he already knew' (1984, p. 90). Goodman reported on how Jonathon, who had been writing stories which anyone could read, came home after one week in school and refused to write anything but his name. 'His response to the question, "Why don't you write a story?" was "I can't write 'til I'm in the first grade," and he didn't' (Goodman, 1980, p. 3). Johns refers to (an example already cited in this book) a seven year old who when asked what reading was said "Stand-up, sit-down". When the youngster was asked to explain what he meant he said that the teacher had him stand up when he read. He would continue reading until he made a mistake and was then asked to sit down. Hence reading was perceived as a stand-up sit-down process' (Johns, 1976, p. 11). Such statements may seem bizarre but is it the case that the situations themselves are bizarre and the children are simply attempting to make sense of them? Perhaps we should, as Hughes and Grieve (1983) suggest: 'no longer treat the child as merely a passive recipient of questions and instruction but must indeed start to view the child as someone who is actively trying to make sense of the situation he is in – however bizarre it may seem' (p. 114).

The evidence suggests that there are many teachers in schools who provide experiences of literacy which make sense only in terms of school instructional practices. Those experiences do not represent a rich, meaningful literacy experience for children and there is little opportunity within such a framework for participation in relevant literacy activities. There is little if any relationship between those experiences and the world outside school, and there is, within such experiences, often little encouragement and much perjorative criticism. Children have to conform to the teachers' model of literacy. The teachers have ownership not only of instruction but also of learning. Children's own ideas about literacy are ignored or rejected. The contrast between the way literacy has been emerging at home and the way it is expected to develop in school could not be greater or more discontinuous.

Criticism of such a kind must be considered within the context of two issues. One is that it must be recognised that schools and homes are inevitably different; they do have different aims and objectives.

In discussing the gap between home and school Tizard and Hughes (1984) point out: 'It may be argued that such a gap is not necessarily a bad thing' (p. 263). They point out that it may be quite justifiable that school, being different, can introduce children to new events and new ways of reflecting on those events. Children must eventually learn to communicate with those who do not share the context of their non-school experiences. Schooling offers children the opportunity to learn to cope with the world in a decontextualised way (a position argued strongly by Donaldson, 1978). School also has, as an environment, different physical and social characteristics, not the least being larger numbers of children and, relatively, fewer adults. Clearly, schools cannot be homes and it is not the intention of this book to argue that they should be. However, it is quite clear that (a) there is a great deal that can be learnt from homes and parents about ways of facilitating intellectual development and, in particular, the emergence of literacy, and (b) that teachers are already interested in establishing relationships between home and school in the area of literacy. They hope, presumably, to avoid perpetuating what Blatchford, Battle and May (1982) call the 'parallel worlds' of home and school. Blatchford et al. comment that the existence of this parallelism 'can lead to missed opportunities; it means that a potentially valuable co-operation is not set in motion – one that would benefit the child, because he would expand his horizons by bringing aspects of the two environments in relation to each other (p. 164).

The proposition of this chapter is not that schools should become homes, but is, in part, that schools should learn to recognise and acknowledge the positive elements that derive from home experiences, and experiences of literacy in particular, and explore school practices to see if there is not room for some of these to become, albeit in a modified form, part of the learning context within school.

The second issue is whether it really matters that children experience discontinuity where literacy is concerned when they begin school. After all, most children learn to read and write. Unfortunately, there are many who do *not* learn to read and write: many can only operate at low levels of efficiency, and some who can read and write choose not to do so. Some teachers of young children seem to be unaware of this. Hodgson and Pryke (1983) say: 'Two infant teachers, one with forty years' experience, said that they did not realise that reading fell away in the early secondary years. One particular lady, who has since retired, said that she thought that once they could do it they went on and on' (p. 43). Meek (1984) has no doubt that the way children are introduced to literacy in school can have a profound effect on their life-long view of reading. She says: 'If we have learnt anything in the last ten years about reading it is that children's earliest encounters with books and print characterise for them what reading is. Recent research makes it clear that the first things teachers tell children determine how subsequent information about reading is interpreted' (p. 42). Wells (1986) makes a fairly similar point about thinking and language when he says: 'Their introduction to formal learning and the lessons learnt at this stage will influence the whole of their subsequent careers at school' (p. 90) and he goes on to point out that: 'Few, if any teachers would wish their pupils to come to expect that schools are places where their individual initiative in thinking and speaking is disvalued, where the asking of questions is to be left to the teacher, and where the best answer is short and preferably expressed in exactly the words that the teacher already has in mind. Yet ... this seems to be the message of the hidden curriculum' (p. 90). The hidden curriculum where literacy is concerned also 'disvalues' the child's own competence with literacy.

Most of the narrow practices and resulting perverse views of what literacy is can be traced back to the assumptions outlined at the beginning of this book. Once assumptions became entrenched in practices that become conventional, they cease to be reflected upon and tend to take on an axiomatic quality which appears to render them safe from examination. It is not the case that teachers set out to create narrow and bizarre views about literacy, nor is it the case that the failure to examine the consequences of those assumptions is a result of teachers being uncaring or lazy. Many studies of classroom life have shown that teachers of young children, and in particular teachers of literacy (Southgate-Booth, Arnold, and Johnson, 1981), are conscientious and hard-working. Nor is it the case that there are no classrooms where interesting and varied literacy experiences are being created. It is perhaps the extent of teachers' involvement, and the physical and mental demands of that involvement, which prevent them from being able to observe, in a more distanced and reflective way, their literacy practices and the consequences of those practices. Reflective observation is of critical importance. As Downing (1970a) says: 'Children do not always learn what the teacher thinks she is teaching. Therefore, it is important to consider the concealed lessons unintentionally taught by different methods. What may children be learning about the purpose and relevance of reading from such methods as those which require children to learn by rote such rules as, 'When two vowels go out walking the first does the talking?' Many children with such methods must think that reading is some kind of mystic ritual' (p. 9).

If, as Downing suggests, one 'rejects materials or methods which may give children a false impression of the purpose and relevance of reading and writing' (1970a, p. 9), what does one put in their place? The replacement should not simply be an alternative (in an absolute sense that may not be wholly necessary), but provide scope within schooling for a literacy curriculum that recognises the abilities with, and knowledge about, literacy that children bring to school, and allows for the emergence of literacy to continue. It does not mean that children are left to get on with it, nor does it mean that a teacher simply abandons all her existing practices.

This book has never suggested that the emergence of literacy just happens. It was made clear in Chapter 1 that the notion of 'natural' literacy development was not going to be used precisely because it could be seen as implying some kind of biological, maturational model. The stance of this book is decidely interventionist. Literacy cannot emerge in a vacuum. The emergence of literacy demands provision and intervention, and this has been evident from the research examined in Chapters 2, 3 and 4. Parents or other adults provide contexts for the experience, demonstration and practice of literacy. They also intervene in children's experience to discuss, evaluate and develop the literacy base of that experience, and they do so in very sensitive ways. In looking at the development of a context for emergent literacy, school teachers must aim to intervene in similar ways.

This does not mean that teachers should abandon all that they are doing. It is not the intention of this book to claim that particular practices have no place in the curriculum, although those that involve humiliation (and similar phenomena) might be an exception. It is, however, the message of this chapter that teachers should examine their practices to see if they help children understand, as fully as possible, what literacy is. Teachers must ask themselves: Do the literacy-instructional practices in my classroom give a true picture of what literacy is, what it is for, and how it works? If they do not, and the evidence cited already in this chapter suggests that might be the case in many classrooms, then teachers should consider how those practices might be modified, in order to create an environment where literacy, in all its aspects, can emerge and be discussed and reflected upon.

The suggestions that follow in this chapter do not represent a curriculum for emergent literacy. They simply provide some thoughts about contexts which do not operate to reject children's views on literacy, which do not seek to obscure the varied functions and uses of literacy, which do not attempt to inhibit discussion about literacy, which do not hide the relevance of literacy, and, perhaps most of all, which do not disguise the fact that literacy is a social phenomenon that allows people to communicate with each other in purposeful ways.

I would suggest that a context for the continued emergence of literacy would operate to:

- help children understand that literacy is about creating meaning and communicating meaning;

- help children understand that literacy is a distinctly human activity. It enables people to communicate;

- help children see that people engage in literacy acts because such acts are considered important and useful by those people;

- help children recognise that literacy is a means to many kinds of ends – that it serves a wide range of real functions;

- help children understand that literacy acts are pleasurable because they enable the satisfaction of a whole variety of personal needs;

- help children appreciate that their existing achievements in literacy are important and valued;

- provide frequent opportunities for engagement and experiment in relevant and purposeful literacy behaviour;

- provide, wherever possible, activities involving the authentic use of literacy;

- provide space for discussion of, and reflection on, literacy performance.

There are now a range of books which can supply many practical examples that, in various ways and to various degrees, meet the above criteria. Holdaway (1979); Butler and Turbill (1984); Turbill (1982 and 1983); Goodman (1986); Graves (1983); Hansen, Newkirk and Graves (1985); Waterland (1985); Walshe (1981); Bennett (1979); Newkirk and Atwell (1982); Meek (1981); Newman (1984); Moon (1985); and Raban (1985) do not all share exactly the same stance, but do begin to offer strategies which help children develop a more valid sense of what literacy is. For more specific practices these books are good guides.

In a more general sense, however, there are three aspects which are critical if the emergence of literacy is to be continuous. There must be an environment where literacy has a high profile and status; there must be access to valid demonstrations of literacy; and opportunity to engage in purposeful literacy acts which are acknowledged as valid literacy behaviour. All of these must allow space and provision for discussion and reflection. None of those aspects is meant to be mutually exclusive. Indeed it is impossible to find examples which fit neatly into only one of those categories. They are, however, useful as starting points to discuss the creation of a school context for the continued emergence of literacy.

A high profile for literacy

Access to understanding literacy is easier if one is in a situation where the status of literacy is high and its value is reinforced by frequent occurrence. It is salutory to compare the richness and complexity of the outside-school print environment with that inside the classroom. Too many classrooms are almost devoid of print save for a few fading labels, some shabby books, and plenty of teacher captions. It is not uncommon to find infant classrooms with no book corners. In one reception class where there were no books on display I was told: 'The children can get a library book once a week from the school library.' Fortunately most classrooms are considerably better than that one – but teachers, in both nursery and infant classrooms, might like to compare their classrooms against the following list which is adapted from a 'Survey of displayed literacy indicators' (Loughlin, Cole, and Sheehan, cit. in Ivener, 1983).

Messages about the current day
Are there schedules, assignments, notices, timetables, announcements, results, relating to the current day? How many are child initiated?

Functional labels
Are there working labels on holders, cupboards or equipment that supply information about contents or manner of use? Are the labels clean and legible? Were they written by children or the teacher?

Child written or child dictated work
How much of this is there? How much of it is less than one week old? How much of it is over a month old? Have the children displayed it themselves?

Explanatory labels
Are exhibits and displays accompanied by print that explains or amplifies the materials displayed? Is this print written by children or the teacher?

Displayed directions for activities
Are there cards, charts or notices that allow children to work independently? Are they child or teacher initiated? Can the children add to them or alter them?

Record collection
Are there any charts or sheets which call for children to record information? Are these child or teacher constructed and do the children record it themselves?

Instruments for recording language
Are there child accessible collections of pencils, pens, crayons, chalks, paper, envelopes, booklets, chalkboards, as well as tape-recorders and typewriters? Do the children have to ask permission to use them?

Places for recording and using language
Are there spaces for writing and reading? Are they quiet or separate from other areas? Are appropriate materials stored in, or by, these areas? Who determines when the children can use these areas?

References
Are there lists, pictures, charts, books, directories, catalogues and other reference sources available for ongoing activities?

Imaginative play
Does the imaginative play area (e.g. the home corner) have relevant and accessible literacy materials?

World-related print
Do the children engage in activities which involve newspapers, magazines, TV papers, phone books, cookery books, shopping lists, other lists,

food labels and packets, diaries and calendars, tickets, programmes, posters, etc? Do the children initiate these activities and do they bring the material in?

Books with covers or pages displayed
How many books have covers clearly visible or have pages open to display at levels where they can be reached or read? Have the children or the teacher displayed them? Are the books near appropriate displays?

Book provision
How many non-reading scheme books are there? How many are damaged? How many have been published in the last three years? How many are fiction and how many are non-fiction? Are there comics and newspapers in the library corner? Who selects books for the library corner?

Display spaces
Are there adequate areas where children can mount and display their own work and notices? Are there tools for display and mounting available for the children's use?

The questions fall into two types: questions about the provision and questions to do with ownership and control. The above categories are not complete by any means and omit some aspects which will be discussed later. They do, however, give a portrait of the potential print dynamism of a classroom. A classroom which is rich in print, where print is used to control and regulate many aspects of behaviour, where there is a constant turnover of print, where print from the outside world is used in the classroom, where there are plenty of opportunities to make and use print, and where children control many of the things they produce and do things with what they produce, is a classroom which has the potential to help children understand that print is a vital and relevant part of classroom experience, and enables the emergence of literacy to occur continuously. Print and space, however, are of little value if they are not in constant use, and if that use is not accompanied by discussion and reflection.

Given that experience of literacy does not simply involve being familiar with objects or labels, but means actually using print, the provision of demonstrations is of particular importance.

DEMONSTRATIONS OF LITERACY

The richness of the demonstrations available in the non-school world contrasts vividly with those available inside the classroom. Children can hardly fail to understand that some school activities are important. Literacy clearly belongs in this category. Literacy-related activities occupy a large part of any schoolchild's day, and directly, or indirectly, they reinforce the understanding that the teacher considers them to be important.

There are, however, some very mixed messages for children experiencing conventional literacy instruction. What do the children see when they observe the behaviour of the major figure in the class – the teacher? Do they, in fact, see an adequate image of a literate adult? Do they see an image of an adult who treats literacy as something of personal importance? Do they see a person who reads frequently and for a wide range of purposes? Is there a good match between what teachers say about literacy and what they actually do with literacy? The answer is, too often, 'no' and it is easy to see why so many children have odd ideas about literacy; see literacy in schools as being irrelevant, purposeless and unrelated to non-school life; or see it as something to be done only for the teacher's sake.

Children do see teachers read and write – but what kind of messages are being conveyed to the children about the literacy being employed? Almost all the reading and writing that teachers engage in within their classroom shares one particular feature: the activities are performed for the sake of instruction. Literacy instruction is, of course, a major and valid purpose of schooling. But instruction is not the only purpose of literacy and those other purposes are going to be obscured from children whose perception of literacy within school is gleaned from the activities carried out by teachers. Teachers know that literacy is a means to an end. For a child observing literacy behaviour in classrooms those ends are difficult to see. It is only too easy to understand why so many children believe that schooling is an end in itself.

I asked a large group of students to observe infant teachers during visits to schools and record teacher literacy-related behaviours. We found that story-reading occurred, but with quite a range of frequency, both within and across schools. Some children had stories several times a day, some only once a week. We found very little reading aloud of children's work. It was usually only special pieces which were so honoured. There was much writing on the blackboard, usually at the start of lessons – although later additions were made, usually spellings. Marking was carried out and children were heard to read. There was, occasionally, some searching for information. With the exception of reading records it seemed as if record-keeping was done out of sight of the children, and any personal reading was carried out in staffrooms. Incidentally, it was extremely rare to find any use of print from the non-school world (except sometimes in 'shops'), and not a single instance of a newspaper or television magazine could be found (except covering painting tables).

Clearly the notions of, and understandings about, literacy that may emerge in such classrooms might be extremely narrow and possibly distorted. Such a print-world and such print-related behaviour bears virtually no apparent relationship to the print-world experienced by children prior to schooling. There is much evidence to show that classrooms do not have to operate like this and that teachers can provide demonstrations of literacy which open up rather than close down children's perceptions of literacy.

Booth and Hall (1986) used demonstrations to help hearing-impaired children become more aware of some of the ways in which literacy can be used for life purposes. Teachers, in front of the children, read newspapers and magazines, ordered equipment, answered letters, and acted out roles in restaurants by taking orders and creating menus. Teachers are unfortunately so often concerned with making children work that they cease doing interesting things themselves in classrooms. As May (1982) said of teachers: 'They're often so busy teaching reading that they don't take the time to read' (p. 223). Teachers do not always appreciate that there are aspects of their own work which, although usually hidden from children, could provide very interesting demonstrations of how literacy functions. A perfect example was recorded by Martin (1976). A teacher was sitting in a nursery class entering recent events into the school log book. The following conversation took place:

Andrew: What are you writing?

Miss E: Some of the interesting things that have happened here in the nursery.

Andrew: Tell me them.

Miss E: This one says, 'Mrs Taylor and Mrs Shotton (local Inspectors) visited the nursery during the afternoon session to see the climbing frame and make arrangements for its removal.'

Andrew: What did they want to look at it for? Drew says they're going to take it away on a lorry.

Miss E: I'm hoping so. It's very rusty and dangerous for you to use. That's why I asked Mrs Shotton to come and see it. Then, after she had been here I wrote about it in this book.

Andrew: Read some more.

Miss E: 'The nursery school closed for the October holidays.'

Andrew: The writing's different. Why?

Miss E: Mrs Tindale wrote those two pages. You see, I was poorly and had to stay at home.

Andrew: Is that in?

Miss E: Yes, here it is.

Andrew: What are the numbers for?

Miss E: That is the date. It tells us the exact day it happened.

Andrew: Is it a true story?

Miss E: Everything in here is true. I only write down the things that actually happen.

Andrew: Do you ever write down about the boys and girls?

Miss E: Often. Let's find some. This one tells us about the day we all went to Stanley Zoo. Here is the one about Diane and the day she cut her eye and had to be taken to hospital.

Andrew: It a nice story book. Why have you never read it to us?

What a good question! This dialogue exemplifies so many of the things said so far about the emergence of literacy at home. The interaction, which is child initiated, takes place because the adult is doing something that looks intrinsically interesting. Throughout the conversation it is the child who leads the way; the child asks all the questions. The teacher, however, sensitively brings the conversation back to the book in her third answer. The child demonstrates genuine intellectual enquiry, 'Is it all real?' The child also reveals some knowledge of his own. He talks appropriately about 'writing' and 'numbers' and notices that the writing has changed at one point. The teacher pitches her answers at a comprehensible level. It is a typical home-type literacy engagement, except that it took place in a school. The discussion is reminiscent of the conversation undertaken by Pauline and her mother about their shopping list which was referred to in Chapter 2. In both cases the actual behaviour provoked a number of issues which had the capacity to enlarge the child's understanding of how literacy works. Andrew's final question is a very important one: Why not involve the children in these aspects of teachers' work? How often do teachers talk to children about their own interests in reading and writing, or bring in print which interests them? How often do teachers write with children, read their own work and subject it to scrutiny by the children? Do teachers have to hide, or keep apart, their literacy behaviours? One of my students wanted to help a reception class understand that written language could be modified once written. She arranged for a message from the head teacher which demanded a reply. Together she and the class drafted a reply which kept being altered as better phrases and sentences were found. When the teacher finally asked, 'Is it OK now?' one child said, 'You can't send that to Mr Gibson, he'll kill you!' A rich and very meaningful discussion followed.

Concern for demonstrations need not be confined to teacher behaviour. There are other people in schools who use print and many others can be persuaded to appear. There is, however, another source of demonstrations, although it might be more accurate to say a 'possible' source. It is something of a paradox that books, and in particular reading schemes, should show so few examples of people reading and writing for any purpose. Such materials again, in some respects, operate to close down understandings about literacy rather than open them up. Studies in America (Parker, 1979; Snyder, 1979; D'Angelo, 1983; and Green-Wilder and Kingston, 1986) and in Britain (Hall, 1983) show that too many reading schemes hardly ever show literacy in action. Hall (1983) felt able to say that the message of books in reading schemes 'to judge from the way that reading is portrayed, is that reading is a marginal activity, not very functional, highly school based, and not particularly pleasurable; all the attributes of a low status activity' (p. 31). To use 'real' books as an alternative to reading schemes does not leave a teacher any better off (Hall, 1985); they also have very few images of people reading. Writing fares even less well than reading. Such messages are surely not the ones intended by editors, writers and publishers, but are they the messages that children actually get from the demonstrations offered?

Although 'real' books may not carry many demonstrations of literacy, they can play a major role in teacher demonstrations of literate behaviour. Such an approach is a central feature of Holdaway's (1979) shared-book experience. The teacher when reading books to the children or in sharing reading with them can present a very effective image of a book user. Not only can the teacher show how many of the conventions of reading operate, but can also show through the frequency with which books are shared, and the excitement and interest with which they are shared, that reading has considerable value and status.

Being in an environment where literacy has high status and where there are appropriate demonstrations will still be limiting unless there are ample opportunities to actually engage in a wide range of literacy practices where the performances are valued.

ENGAGEMENT IN LITERACY

There are few areas of life to which literacy cannot relate. In their lives prior to schooling, children will not only have witnessed a wide range of literacy acts but will also have taken part in many of them. Before schooling children are able to participate in literacy used for the purpose of living. As literacy continues to emerge so their involvement increases. The examples discussed in Chapters 3 and 4 reveal many children reading and writing for a wide range of purposes, including pleasure. Equally important are the responses of adults when they treat children's efforts as genuine communication. In those pre-school days opportunities for valued literacy engagement are frequent.

It will be clear that engagement in literacy does not mean the rote practice of so-called skills. Engagement in literacy means, as far as possible, engagement in acts which fulfil the criteria for genuine non-school literacy acts. That is, acts where literacy is a means to a non-literate end, or where personal satisfaction and enjoyment guide the nature of the act. Teachers who keep diaries of their own literacy activities will find that they can usefully compare the results not only with their own activities in school but also with the children's. The difference is likely to be just as dramatic. The evidence discussed in the first half of this chapter showed that in too many classrooms young children's freedom to engage in meaningful literacy acts was considerably restricted. A diet of reading from reading schemes and completing handwriting exercises is unlikely to satisfy any need, other than that of the teacher's, for literacy engagement.

There is no shortage of possibilities for interesting and varied engagements in literacy, nor are teachers unaware of these. The problem is that too often such activities are viewed as something special or something different rather than normal, regular and inevitable. I have had many conversations of the type where the response to questions like 'Do the children ever write letters?' is 'Oh yes, we all wrote to X last term'. The teachers' definition is of an event completed rather than of a perpetual opportunity to participate in letter-writing when the child considers it appropriate. It is something of a vicious paradox that we teach children to read and write precisely so that they will be able to participate freely in literacy acts, yet we operate to deny them the free participation in such acts while they are at school.

It is instructive to look back at some of the research already cited in this book. There was Giti (Baghban, 1984) whose parents supplied her with a desk, and a range of writing materials and writing utensils. Giti was able to utilise these whenever she wanted to. She was able to select what appeared to her to be the appropriate materials and use them in the way she wanted. Engaging in literacy was, for her, a constant activity which could be used, as it was by the children in the Schickedanz study (1984), for a whole variety of purposes. The engagements of the children in the Schickedanz study were often of a 'play' kind, but through that play the literacy functioned in an appropriate way: children took notes; made calendars; wrote shopping lists, and kept diaries, just as the children in the Hall *et al.* study (1986) incorporated literacy into restaurant play, home play and office play. In many of these examples the role of adults was important; sometimes as demonstrator, sometimes as initiator, sometimes as participant, sometimes as adviser, and always as a trusted observer and commentator. Is it possible to provide opportunities in classrooms for engagement that match the richness of those available in the print-world outside school? Is it possible to allow children the freedom in school to explore in their own ways the application of literacy? Is it possible to create contexts where the emergence of literacy can occur within a range of either real or realistic purposes?

Clearly it is. In the few days prior to writing this section I saw nursery children playing at running a puppet theatre and a baby clinic. In both cases print became an integral part of the play. The children made use of the freedom they had, the materials available, and the support of adults. Some of the children working on the puppet theatre had been to theatres. They brought in programmes and other print deriving from their visits. The children were soon making tickets, programmes and posters. Finally, and with some adult support, they created a seating plan and numbered the chairs in front of the puppet theatre. The writing was an integral part of the discussion about puppets, the making of puppets and in the performances, which were, everyone agreed, quite unique. The baby clinic had to have, like the one they had visited, a receptionist who spent much time on the phone taking appointments and 'writing' cards. Children in this class had access to an enormous number of facilities for making print, and the utilisation of print in their activities was a normal part of the behaviour. As well as making their own marks children could tell stories, or recount events, to an adult who would type as the children spoke. Thus the children had literacy choices of all kinds. All these children's efforts were valued as products of the intent to create meaning through literate acts. Their efforts were discussed, displayed, and proudly taken home.

In recent weeks I have seen or talked to teachers who have set up and documented in their reception classes, airports, estate agents, publishing houses, newspaper offices, hospitals, and secretaries' offices. In all cases the children made extensive use of print – both for reading and for writing. In all these cases it was the children who controlled the use of literacy and decided what was appropriate.

The events mentioned so far derive in some way from teacher initiation but if children have freedom to use literacy they will create their own events. The teachers' dispute in England during 1985–6 was widely seen as having a totally negative impact on children. However, there were positive aspects. In one reception class the frequency of lesson cancellation resulted in some children creating messages for other children to remind them what was happening, where they needed to be and what they had to bring or take. Thus the literate experience was at the root of authentic action, and that action was unknown to the teacher until it was discovered later pinned up on the wall.

Schools themselves offer numerous opportunities for literacy engagements but, as in the last example, the children's responses need to be treated seriously. Harste, Woodward and Burke (1984) reported how they persuaded one kindergarten teacher to allow her children to sign in every day. The children enthusiastically made marks. The teacher's response was: 'This isn't working. The children aren't writing' (p. 15). If the children's responses can be valued then the school day can become a sequence of literacy acts. Even the youngest children can sign in and sign up for all kinds of activities; they can produce their own notices for parents and events; they can collect and put up dinner menus; they can read their classroom timetables; they can write invitations to school parties; they can construct and use their own notice boards; they can write messages to other teachers; they can help the headteacher or school secretary with opening mail; they can even leave messages for cleaners. Anning (1984) says of the children in her school: 'Our children have also learnt that adults in the school will read cryptic messages – in a hectic modern household there must be plenty of real life examples of this for them to see – and polite instructions to the cleaners or teaching staff such as "Ples liv this model to dry" or "Dunt forget pe today" are heeded.'

In her school, Anning provided many contexts where literacy was at the heart of apparently more important objectives. One class of six year olds was due to move into a new classroom. The children were given the equipment catalogues, selected what they wanted, filled in the order forms and then worked with what they had bought. The consequence of treating children's efforts seriously means that you have to accept what happens. Thus that class ordered some things that the teachers would not have ordered but which turned out to be well-used. Other classes planned days out. The children chose where to go, found out how to get there, planned within a budget, budgeted and shopped for food and made their lunches. They wrote for timetables, collected and accounted for money and finally went on their visit. The entire operation was carried out by the children, all decisions being debated and agreed by the class. Anning told the author that she found that these children treated the task very seriously and in the process learnt an enormous amount about the way people use literacy.

The emphasis so far has been on what might be termed 'functional literacy', but of equal importance are the opportunities for engaging in literacy for pleasure where children can also control aspects of the literacy acts. Classrooms should be places where children can choose to read, and where reading is not only an activity to be done when 'real' work is finished. Reading with understanding and for pleasure is real work.

Children should never need to ask if they can engage in purposeful literacy acts. If a classroom provides an environment where the status of literacy is high, where there are powerful demonstrations of literacy and where children can freely engage in literacy, then children will take every opportunity to use their knowledge and abilities to act in a literate way. If one adds the other two aspects mentioned earlier – those of discussion and reflection – to the three identified above, then there is less likelihood of a discontinuity between what emerges prior to schooling and what will emerge after schooling has begun. The emergence of literacy can continue in the same way it began – with the expectation that written language makes sense.

CONCLUSION

The areas outlined in the second part of this chapter represent a starting point for thinking about the construction of an environment in school where valid understandings about literacy can continue to emerge. The conclusion of this book has to be that such an environment is likely to be the most successful one at helping children to become readers and writers because it is an environment which comes closest to replicating the positive experiences that many children have prior to school. Literacy seems to emerge in contexts which enable children to experience language as a totally meaningful phenomenon. Within such contexts the expectations children have about print making sense are affirmed. It is through knowing what written language can do that children gain control over its form. Harste, Woodward and Burke (1984) claim that it is because children are readers and writers that they are able to increasingly control the form of written language, not vice versa. It is because in the first instance children are exposed to a world where written language makes sense and is used in meaningful ways that children are able to generate understandings about how it works. The emergence of literacy is a fact not a fiction and provided children are given appropriate opportunities to display their knowledge they are only too ready to give demonstrations. What schools must do is allow them the chance to do so and not refute their hard-won, and generally reasonable, assumptions about written language. Children have an extraordinary capacity for making sense of their experience. We must not present them with a narrow and distorted world of literacy in which making sense is almost impossible.

Bibliography

ANDERSON, A. and STOKES, S. (1984) 'Social and institutional influences on the development and practice of literacy' in GOELMAN, H., OBERG, A. and SMITH, F. (eds.) *Awakening to Literacy*. London: Heinemann Educational Books.

ANNING, A. (1984) 'Reading and writing to some purpose', *Child Education*, 61, 1, pp. 26–7.

AYERS, D. and DOWNING, J. (1982) 'Testing children's concepts of reading', *Educational Research*, 24, 4, pp. 277–83.

BAGHBAN, M. (1984) *Our Daughter Learns to Read and Write: A Case Study from Birth to Three*. Newark, Delaware: International Reading Association.

BENNETT, J. (1979) *Learning to Read with Picture Books*. Gloucester: Thimble Press.

BENNETT, N., DESFORGES, C., COCKBURN, A. and WILKINSON, B. (1984) *The Quality of Pupil Learning Experiences*. Hillsdale, New Jersey: Lawrence Erlbaum Associates.

BISSEX, G. (1980) *Gnys at Wrk: A Child Learns to Read and Write*. Cambridge, Mass.: Harvard University Press.

BISSEX, G. (1984) 'The child as a teacher', in GOELMAN, H., OBERG, A. and SMITH, F. (eds.) *Awakening to Literacy*. London: Heinemann Educational Books.

BLATCHFORD, P., BATTLE, S. and MAY, J. (1982) *The First Transition: Home to Pre-school*. Slough: NFER/Nelson.

BOOTH, E. and HALL, N. (1986) 'Making sense of literacy', in HUSTLER, D., CASSIDY, T. and CUFF, E. (eds.) *Action Research in Classrooms and Schools*. London: Allen and Unwin.

BRUNER, J. (1983) *Child Talk*. Oxford: Oxford University Press.

BUTLER, A. and TURBILL, J. (1984) *Towards a Reading-Writing Classroom*. Rozelle, NSW: Primary English Teaching Association.

CAZDEN, C. (1983) 'Adult assistance to language development: scaffolds, models and direct instruction', in PARKER, R. and DAVIS, F. (eds.) *Developing Literacy: Young Children's Use of Literacy*. Newark, Delaware: International Reading Association.

CLARK, M. M. (1976) *Young Fluent Readers*. London: Heinemann Educational Books.

CLAY, M. (1972) *Sand*. London: Heinemann Educational Books.

CLAY, M. (1975) *What Did I Write?* London: Heinemann Educational Books.

CLAY, M. (1979a) *Stones.* London: Heinemann Educational Books.

CLAY, M. (1979b) *Reading: The Patterning of Complex Behaviour.* London: Heinemann Educational Books.

CLAY, M. (1979c) *The Early Detection of Reading Difficulties: A Diagnostic Survey with Recovery Procedures.* London: Heinemann Educational Books.

CLAY, M. (1982) *Observing Young Readers.* London: Heinemann Educational Books.

COCHRAN-SMITH, M. (1984) *The Making Of A Reader.* Norwood, New Jersey: Ablex Publishing Corporation.

COLTHEART, M. (1979) 'When can children learn to read – and when can they be taught?' in WALLER, T. G. and MACKINNON, G. E. (eds.) *Reading Research: Advances in Theory and Practice,* Vol. 1. New York: Academic Press.

CRAGO, M. and CRAGO, H. (1983) *Prelude to Literacy: A Pre-School Child's Encounter with Picture and Story.* Carbondale, Ill.: Southern Illinois University Press.

CURTIS, J. (1984) 'A teacher's role in Natural Language acquisition'. Paper presented at Annual Conference of California Teachers of English, San Jose.

D'ANGELO, K. (1983) 'Biblio-power: promoting reading and writing with books', *Reading Psychology,* 3, 4, pp. 347–54.

DAWSON, A. (1984) 'Pre-reading skills and environmental awareness', *Bulletin of Environmental Education,* No. 163, pp. 18–19.

DES (1975) *A Language for Life* (The Bullock Report). London: HMSO.

DES (1982) *Education 5 to 9: an illustrative survey of 80 first schools in England.* London: HMSO.

DIEHL-FAXON, J. and DOCKSTADER-ANDERSON, K. (1985) 'Discourse intonation patterns of mothers reading to their young children – readerese?', in NILES, J. and LALIK, R. (eds.) *Issues in Literacy: A Research Perspective.* New York: National Reading Conference.

DOMAN, G. (1985) *Teach Your Baby to Read.* London: Jonathan Cape.

DONALDSON, M. (1978) *Children's Minds.* London: Fontana Books.

DONALDSON, M. (1984) 'Speech and writing and modes of learning', in GOELMAN, H., OBERG, A. and SMITH, F. (eds.) *Awakening to Literacy.* London: Heinemann Educational Books.

DOWNING, J. (1969a) 'How children think about reading', *The Reading Teacher,* 23, 3, pp. 217–30.

DOWNING, J. (1969b) 'The perception of linguistic structure in learning to read', *British Journal of Educational Psychology,* 39, pp. 267–71.

DOWNING, J. (1970a) 'Relevance versus ritual in learning to read', *Reading,* 4, 2, pp. 4–12.

DOWNING, J. (1970b) 'Children's concepts of language in learning to read', *Educational Research,* 12, pp. 106–12.

DOWNING, J. (1972) 'Children's developing concepts of spoken and written language', *Journal of Reading Behaviour,* 4, 1, pp. 1–19.

DOWNING, J. (1979) *Reading and Reasoning.* Edinburgh: W. & C. Black.

DOWNING, J., AYERS, D. and SCHAFFER, B. (1982) 'Conceptual and perceptual factors in learning to read', *Educational Research*, 21, 1, pp. 11–17.

DOWNING, J., AYERS, D. and SCHAFFER, B. (1984) *The Linguistic Awareness in Reading Readiness Test*. Slough: NFER/Nelson.

DOWNING, J. and OLIVER, P. (1974) 'The child's concept of a word', *Reading Research Quarterly*, 9, 4, pp. 568–82.

DOWNING, J., OLLILA, L. and OLIVER, P. (1975) 'Cultural differences in children's concepts of reading and writing', *British Journal of Educational Psychology*. 45, pp. 312–16.

DOWNING, J., OLLILA, L. and OLIVER, P. (1977) 'Concepts of language in children from differing socio-economic backgrounds', *Journal of Educational Research*, 70, pp. 277–81.

DURKIN, D. (1966) *Children Who Read Early*. New York: Teacher's College Press.

DYSON, A. H. (1985a) 'Individual differences in emerging writing', in FARR, M. (ed.) *Children's Early Writing Development*. Norwood, New Jersey: Ablex Publishing Corporation.

DYSON, A. H. (1985b) 'Three emergent writers and the school curriculum: copying and other myths', *The Elementary School Journal*, 85, 4, pp. 497–512.

ELKIND, B. (1981) 'Stages in the development of reading', in SIGEL, I., BRODZINSKY, D. and GOLINKOFF, R. (eds.) *New Directions in Piagetian Theory and Practice*. Hillsdale, New Jersey: Lawrence Erlbaum Associates.

EVANECHKO, P., OLLILA, L., DOWNING, J. and BRAUN, C. (1973) 'An investigation of the reading readiness domain', *Research into the Teaching of English*, 7, pp. 61–78.

FERREIRO, E. and TEBEROSKY, A. (1983) *Literacy Before Schooling*. London: Heinemann Educational Books.

FITTS, P. and POSNER, M. (1967) *Human Performance*. Belmont, California: Brooks-Cole.

FORESTER, A. (1977) 'What teachers can learn from natural readers', *The Reading Teacher*, 31, pp. 160–6.

FOX, C. (1983) 'Talking like a book: young children's oral monologues', in MEEK, M. (ed.) *Opening Moves*. London: University of London.

FOX, C. (1985) 'The book that talks', *Language Arts*, 62, 4, pp. 374–84.

GATTEGNO, C. (1969) *Reading with Words in Colour*. Reading: Educational Explorers.

GIBSON, E. (1970) 'The ontology of reading', *American Psychologist*, 25, 2, pp. 136–43.

GODDARD, N. (1958) *Reading in the Modern Infant School*. London: University of London.

GODDARD, N. (1974) *Literacy: Language Experience Approaches*. London: Macmillan.

GOLLASCH, F. V. (1982) *Language and Literacy: The Selected Writings of Kenneth S. Goodman*, Vol. 1 and Vol. 2. London: Routledge and Kegan Paul.

GOODALL, M. (1984) 'Can four year olds read words in the environment?', *The Reading Teacher*, 37, 6, pp. 478–82.

GOODMAN, K. (1976a) 'Manifesto for a reading revolution', in DOUGLASS, M. (ed.) *40th Year Book of the Claremont Reading Conference.* Claremont: Claremont Graduate School.

GOODMAN, K. (1976b) 'Linguistically sound research in reading', in FARR, R., NEINTRAUB, S. and TONE, B. (eds.) *Improving Reading Research.* Newark, Delaware: International Reading Association.

GOODMAN, K. (1985) 'Growing into literacy', *Prospects*, 15, 1, pp. 57–65.

GOODMAN, K. (1986) *What's Whole in Whole Language?* Portsmouth, New Jersey: Heinemann Educational Books.

GOODMAN, K. and GOODMAN, Y. (1979) 'Learning to read is natural', in RESNICK, L. and WEAVER, P. (eds.) *Theory and Practice of Early Reading*, Vol. 1. Hillsdale, New Jersey: Lawrence Erlbaum Associates.

GOODMAN, K., GOODMAN, Y. and BURKE, C. (1978) 'Reading for life: the psycholinguistic base', in HUNTER-GRUNDIN, E. and GRUNDIN, H. (eds.) *Reading: Implementing the Bullock Report.* London: Ward Lock Educational.

GOODMAN, Y. (1980) 'The roots of literacy', in DOUGLASS, M. P. (ed.) *Reading: A Humanising Experience.* Claremont: Claremont Graduate School.

GOODMAN, Y. (1981) 'Test review: concepts about print tests', *The Reading Teacher*, 34, pp. 445–8.

GOODMAN, Y. (1983) 'Beginning reading development: strategies and principles', in PARKER, R. and DAVIS, F. (eds.) *Developing Literacy: Young Children's Use of Language.* Newark, Delaware: International Reading Association.

GOODMAN, Y. (1984) 'The development of initial literacy', in GOELMAN, H., OBERG, A. and SMITH, F. (eds.) *Awakening to Literacy.* London: Heinemann Educational Books.

GOODMAN, Y. (1985) 'Kidwatching: observing children in the classroom', in JAGGAR, A. and SMITH-BURKE, M. T. (eds.) *Observing the Language Learner.* Newark, Delaware: International Reading Association.

GOODMAN, Y. and ALTWERGER, B. (1980) 'Reading: how does it begin?' in PINNEL, G. S. (ed.) *Discovering Language With Children.* NCTE.

GOODMAN, Y. and ALTWERGER, B. (1981) *Print Awareness in Pre-School Children: A Working Paper.* Arizona Centre For Research And Development, University of Arizona.

GOULD, T. (1978) *Home Guide to Early Reading.* London: Sphere Books Ltd.

GRAVES, D. (1978) 'We won't let them write', *Language Arts*, 55, pp. 635–40.

GRAVES, D. (1983) *Writing: Teachers and Children at Work.* London: Heinemann Educational Books.

GREEN-WILDER, J. and KINGSTON, A. (1986) 'The depiction of reading in five popular basal series', *The Reading Teacher*, 40, pp. 399–402.

GUNDLACH, R., MCLANE, J., STOTT, F. and MCNAMEE, G. (1985) 'The social foundations of children's early writing development', in FARR, M. (ed.) *Children's Early Writing Development*. Norwood, New Jersey: Ablex Publishing Corporation.

HALL, N. (1983) 'The status of "reading" in reading schemes', *Education* 3-13, 11, 2, pp. 27–32.

HALL, N. (1985) 'Reading about "reading" ', *Reading Horizons*, 25, 2, pp. 103–6.

HALL, N., MAY, L., MOORES, J., SHEARER, J. and WILLIAMS, S. (1986) 'Literacy events in the "home" corner of a nursery school'. Paper given at the World Congress On Reading, London.

HALLIDAY, M. K. (1973) *Explorations in the Function of Language*. London: Edward Arnold.

HANSEN, J., NEWKIRK, T. and GRAVES, D. (1985) *Breaking Ground: Teachers Relate Reading and Writing in the Elementary School*. Portsmouth, New Jersey: Heinemann Educational Books.

HARSTE, J., BURKE, C. and WOODWARD, V. (1982) 'Children's language and world: initial encounters with print', in LANGER, J. and SMITH-BURKE, M. T. (eds.) *Reader Meets Author: Bridging the Gap*. Newark Delaware: International Reading Association.

HARSTE, J., WOODWARD, V. and BURKE, C. (1984) *Language Stories and Literacy Lessons*. Portsmouth, New Hampshire: Heinemann Educational Books.

HARTLEY, D. and QUINE, P. (1982) 'A critical appraisal of Marie Clay's "Concepts about print" test', *Reading*, 16, 2, pp. 109–12.

HAUSSLER, M. (1984) *Transitions into Literacy: A Working Paper*. Arizona: Arizona Centre for Research and Development, University of Arizona.

HAUSSLER, M. (1985) 'A young child's developing concepts of print', in JAGGER, A. and SMITH-BURKE, M. T. (eds.) *Observing the Language Learner*. Newark, Delaware: International Reading Association.

HEATH, S. B. (1982) 'What no bedtime story means', *Language and Society*, 2, pp. 49–76.

HEATH, S. B. (1983) *Ways With Words: Language, Life, and Work in Communities and Classrooms*. Cambridge: Cambridge University Press.

HENDERSON, E. (1980) 'Developmental concepts of word', in HENDERSON, E. and BEERS, J. (eds.) *Developmental and Cognitive Aspects of Learning to Spell: A Reflection of Word Knowledge*. Newark, Delaware: International Reading Association.

HENDERSON, E. and BEERS, J. (1980) *Developmental and Cognitive Aspects of Learning to Spell: A Reflection of Word Knowledge*. Newark, Delaware: International Reading Association.

HIEBERT, E. (1981) 'Developmental patterns and interrelationships of pre-school children's print awareness', *Reading Research Quarterly*, 16, 2, pp. 236–59.

HODGSON, J. and PRYKE, D. (1983) *Reading Competence at 6 and 10*. Shropshire: Shropshire County Council.

HOLDAWAY, D. (1979) *The Foundations of Literacy*. Gosford, NSW: Scholastic.

HOSKISSON, K. (1979) 'Learning to read naturally', *Language Arts*, 56, 5, pp. 489–96.

HUGHES, M. and GRIEVE, R. (1983) 'On asking children bizarre questions', in DONALDSON, M., GRIEVE, R. and PRATT, C. (eds.) *Early Childhood Development and Education*. Oxford: Blackwell.

IREDELL, H. (1898) 'Eleanor learns to read', *Education*, 19, pp. 233–8.

IVENER, B. (1983) 'Inservice: a teacher chosen direction for creating environments for literacy', *The New Mexico Journal of Reading*, 3, 2, pp. 7–12.

JOHNS, J. (1976/7) 'Reading is "stand-up, sit-down"', *Journal of the New England Reading Association*, 12, 1, pp. 10–14.

JONES, M. and HENDRICKSON, N. (1970) 'Recognition by pre-school children of advertised products and book covers', *Journal of Home Economics*, 62, 4, pp. 263–7.

JULIEBO, M. (1985) 'The literacy world of five young children', *Reading-Canada-Lecture*, 3, 2, pp. 126–36.

KAMMLER, B. (1984) 'Ponch writes again: a child at play', *Australian Journal of Reading*, 7, 2, pp. 61–70.

KASTLER, L. A. (1984) 'The sensitivity of kindergarten children to form, function and use of written language'. Paper presented at National Reading Conference, Florida.

KRIPPNER, S. (1963) 'The boy who read at 18 months', *Exceptional Children*, October.

LASS, B. (1982) 'Portrait of my son as an early reader', *The Reading Teacher*, 36, 1, pp. 20–8.

LEICHTER, H. J. (1984) 'Families as environments for literacy', in GOELMAN, H., OBERG, A. and SMITH, F. (eds.) *Awakening to Literacy*. London: Heinemann Educational Books.

MCGEE, L., LOMAX, R. and HEAD, M. (1984) 'Young children's functional reading'. Paper presented at The National Reading Conference, Florida.

MALICKY, G. and NORMAN, C. (1985) 'Reading processes in natural readers', *Reading-Canada-Lecture*, 3, 1, pp. 8–20.

MARTIN, N. (1976) 'Encounters with models', *English in Education*, 10, pp. 9–15.

MASON, G. (1965) 'Children learn words from commercial TV', *Elementary School Journal*, 65, pp. 318–20.

MASON, J. (1980) 'When do children begin to read: an exploration of four year old children's word reading competencies', *Reading Research Quarterly*, 15, 2, pp. 203–27.

MAY, F. (1982) *Reading as Communication*. New York: Charles Merrill Pub. Corp.

MEEK, M. (1981) *Learning to Read*. London: The Bodley Head.

MEEK, M. (1984) 'Turning the key', *Times Educational Supplement*, 29 June, 41.

MILZ, V. (1985) 'First-grader's uses for writing', in JAGGER, A. and SMITH-BURKE, T. (eds.) *Observing the Language Learner*. Newark, Delaware: International Reading Association.

MOON, C. (1985) *Practical Ways to Teach Reading*. London: Ward Lock Educational.

MOON, C. and WELLS, C. G. (1979) 'The influence of home on learning to read', *Journal of Research in Reading*, 2, pp. 53–62.

NEWKIRK, T. and ATWELL, N. (1982) *Understanding Writing: Ways Of Observing, Learning and Teaching*. Chelmsford, Massachusetts: North-East Regional Exchange.

NEWMAN, J. (1984) *The Craft of Children's Writing*. New York: Scholastic Book Services.

PARKER, L. (1979) 'Reading as an activity and theme in children's books', in SHAPIRO, J. (ed.) *Using Literature and Poetry Effectively*. Newark, Delaware: International Reading Association.

PAYTON, S. (1984) *Developing Awareness of Print: A Young Child's First Steps Towards Literacy*. Birmingham: Educational Review.

POSTMAN, N. (1970) 'The politics of reading', in KEDDIE, N. (ed.) *Tinker Tailor: The Myth of Cultural Deprivation*. Harmondsworth: Penguin.

QUIGG, P. (1985) 'The emergence of literacy', *Reading-Canada-Lecture*, 3, 3, pp. 211–17.

RABAN, B. (1985) *Practical Ways to Teach Writing*. London: Ward Lock Educational.

READ, C. (1970) 'Pre-school children's knowledge of English phonology', *Harvard Educational Review*, 41, 1, pp. 1–34.

REID, J. (1958) 'An investigation into thirteen beginners in reading', *Acta Psychologica*, 14, pp. 295–313.

REID, J. (1966) 'Learning to think about reading', *Eductional Research*, 9, pp. 56–62.

SCHICKEDANZ, J. (1984) 'A Study of Literacy Events in the Homes of Six Pre-schoolers'. Paper presented at the National Reading Conference, Florida.

SCHICKEDANZ, J. and SULLIVAN, M. (1984) 'Mom, what does U–F–F spell?' *Language Arts*, 61, 1, pp. 7–17.

SCHIEFFELIN, B. B. and COCHRAN-SMITH, M. (1984) 'Learning to read culturally: literacy before schooling', in GOELMAN, H., OBERG, A. and SMITH, F. (eds.) *Awakening to Literacy*. London: Heinemann Educational Books.

SCHMIDT, E. and YATES, C. (1985) 'Benji learns to read naturally! Naturally Benji learns to read', *Australian Journal of Reading*, 8, 3, pp. 121–34.

SCOLLON, R. and SCOLLON, B. (1981) *Narrative, Literacy and Face in Interethnic Communication*. Norwood, New Jersey: Ablex Publishing Corporation.

SMITH, F. (1971) *Understanding Reading*. New York: Holt, Rinehart and Winston.

SMITH, F. 1976 'Learning to read by reading', *Language Arts*, 53, pp. 297–9, 322.

SMITH, F. (1979) 'The language arts and the learner's mind', *Language Arts*, 56, 2, pp. 118–125.

SMITH, F. (1982) *Writing and the Writer*. London: Heinemann Educational Books.

SNOW, C. (1983) 'Literacy and language: relationships during the preschool years', *Harvard Educational Review*, 53, 2, pp. 165–89.

SNYDER, G. (1979) 'Do basal characters read in their daily lives?' *The Reading Teacher*, 33, 3, pp. 303–6.

SOUTHGATE-BOOTH, V., ARNOLD, H and JOHNSON, S. (1981) *Extending Beginning Reading*. London: Heinemann Educational Books.

STINE, S. (1980) 'Beginning reading naturally', in DOUGLASS, M. P. (ed.) *Reading: A Humanising Experience*. Claremont; Claremont Graduate School.

STREET, B. (1984) *Literacy in Theory and Practice*. Cambridge: Cambridge University Press.

SULZBY, E. (1985) 'Kindergarteners as writers and readers', in FARR, M. (ed.) *Children's Early Writing Development*. Norwood, New Jersey: Ablex Publishing Corporation.

TAWL (1984) *A Kidwatching Guide: Evaluation for Whole Language Classrooms*. Tuscon, Arizona: Arizona Centre for Research and Development.

TAYLOR, D. (1983) *Family Literacy: Young Children Learning to Read and Write*. London: Heinemann Educational Books.

TEALE, W. (1982) 'Towards a theory of how children learn to read and write naturally', *Language Arts*, 59, pp. 555–70.

TEALE, W. (1984) 'Reading to young children: its significance for literacy development', in GOELMAN, H., OBERG, A. and SMITH, F. (eds.) *Awakening to Literacy*. London: Heinemann Educational Books.

THOMPSON, B. (1970) *Learning to Read: A Guide for Parents and Teachers*. London: Sidgwick and Jackson.

THORNDIKE, E. L. (1917) 'Reading as reasoning', *The Journal of Educational Psychology*, 8, pp. 323–32.

TIZARD, B. and HUGHES, M. (1984) *Young Children Learning: Talking and Thinking at Home and School*. London: Fontana.

TORREY, J. (1969) 'Learning to read without a teacher: a case study', *Elementary English*, 46, 5, pp. 550–68.

TORREY, J. W. (1979) 'Reading that comes naturally: the early reader', in WALLER, T. G. and MACKINNON, G. E. (eds.) *Reading Research: Advances in Theory and Practice*. New York: Academic Press.

TOVEY, D. (1976) 'Children's perceptions of reading', *The Reading Teacher*, 29, 536–40.

TURBILL, J. (1982) *No Better Way to Teach Writing*. Sydney: Primary English Teaching Association.

TURBILL, J. (1983) *Now We Want to Write*. Sydney: Primary English Teaching Association.

WALKER, C. (1975) *Teaching Prereading Skills*. London: Ward Lock Educational.

WALSHE, R. D. (1981) *Every Child Can Write.* Sydney: Primary English Teaching Association.

WARDAUGH, R. (1969) 'Theories of reading in relation to beginning reading instruction', *Language Learning,* 21, 1, pp. 1–26.

WATERLAND, L. (1985) *Read With Me: An Apprenticeship Approach to Reading.* Gloucester: Thimble Press.

WELLS, G. (1981) *Learning Through Interaction: The Study of Language Development.* Cambridge: Cambridge University Press.

WELLS, G. (1982) 'Story reading and the development of symbolic skills', *Australian Journal of Reading,* 5, 3, pp. 142–152.

WELLS, G. (1985) 'Pre-school literacy related activities and success in school', in OLSON, G., TORRANCE, N. and HILDYARD, A. (eds.) *Literacy, Language, and Learning: The Nature and Consequences of Reading and Writing.* Cambridge: Cambridge University Press.

WELLS, G. (1986) 'The language experience of five-year old children at home and at school', in COOK-GUMPERZ, J. (ed.) *The Social Construction of Literacy.* Cambridge: Cambridge University Press.

WOLF, R. and TYMITZ, B. (1976) 'Ethnography and schooling: matching enquiry mode to process', *Reading Research Quarterly,* 12, pp. 5–11.

YADEN, D. (1984) 'Reading research in metalinguistic awareness: findings, problems, and classroom applications', *Visible Language,* 18, 1, pp. 5–47.

Index